Thriving

in a Hateful World

Natalie Buske Thomas

ISBN-13: 978-0615933153

ISBN-10: 0615933157

To Brent, Cassandra, Nicholas and
Savannah

AUTHOR'S WORKS

The Serena Wilcox Mysteries

Ruby Red

Project Scarecrow

Bluebird Flown

Covert Coffee

Angels Mark

Camp Conviction

Virtual Memories

Gene Play

Other Books

Fred Born Gifted, The Miracle Dulcimer,
The Magic Camera

Oil Paintings

Most notably *Savannah Reading in the*
Butterfly Garden

www.NatalieBuskeThomas.com

1

PEBBLES IN A JAR

I'm Natalie Buske Thomas, wife and mother of three. I'm an oil painter and an author. I sing. I teach. I volunteer. I've been rejected more times than I have succeeded. I've been envied. I've been stabbed in the back. I've been hurt. I'm disconnected from people who should have loved me, but never did, and never will. I am not alone.

If you've chosen to read this book it's probably because you too feel that you are living in a hateful world. Haters are everywhere, and they do not stop when we are broken. If anything, they smell our vulnerability and they move in for the kill. A book about thriving in a hateful world needs to address what makes us vulnerable to haters.

Sadness can weaken us and make us susceptible to attacks. If there's one thing that I know about, it's loss, and channeling grief into the strength and energy to become a better person. "Thriving in a Hateful World" is about healing and letting go of grief, resentment and toxic baggage. Haters have a difficult time oppressing a healthy, well-adjusted, and hopeful person.

But losses happen, and when they do, even the strongest person can be taken down. While a loss is still fresh, people often say something outrageously inappropriate and hurtful. Long after the hateful words are uttered (and likely forgotten by the people who said them), we still hear them.

That's why I lie low and avoid negative people when I'm feeling broken. I return to my regular social circles only after I've established a position of strength. This is a simple tip that you probably already know, but it's easier said than done, and this strategy doesn't always work. We can't avoid all haters, especially when the haters are people we love! Not every toxic conversation comes out of the mouth of a chronically toxic person. Sometimes we are taken by surprise when a trusted friend or family member says something that cuts us to the core.

People may fail us, so we need multiple strategies to pick ourselves up when we fall down. When I'm struck down by another heartache I ask myself how I can make something good out of something bad. I seek ways to bring honor to the situation.

It wasn't easy to change my natural response to hate and loss. When heartbreaking events are relentless and show no sign of stopping, it is hard to believe that anything is worthwhile. What's the point of anything if everything can be taken away from us in the blink of an eye?

None of us live forever. How can we muster up excitement about living if we know that in the end we're all going to die? I had a choice: I could drag myself through my days feeling defeated or I could fight. When my kids were little and they didn't want to do something, I told them that they had a choice. They could choose to do what I asked with a bad attitude or they could do what I asked with a smile on their face. Doing what I asked was non-negotiable, but their attitude was their choice. This lecture resulted in my children initially doing their best to show me how grumpy they were, but when they realized that their efforts were not going to get them anywhere, they gave up and focused on the task at hand. They mellowed and even adopted a positive attitude. When the task was completed, they were proud of what they had accomplished. I remind myself of this when I don't like what life is demanding of me. Just like my children, if I do what needs to be done, I'll mellow out. Eventually I'll even be proud of what I have achieved.

I've had a fair amount of success in recent years, but only after twenty-plus years of plodding along, hoping for a big break that never did come my way. My progress has been the slow one-pebble-at-a-time variety. This analogy of filling a jar, and being a "pebbler", is what I want to open this book with here in Chapter One. This is my first bit of advice for how to thrive in an unfair and hateful world.

We all have a glass jar that represents our dreams. Imagine that you were born with crystal clear untainted water in a clean sparkly jar. Were you born into family wealth, talent, and a star that shines over your every step? Then your jar may have been nearly full at birth! You can count me out of that group, and since you're reading this book, I'm guessing that you can count yourself out of that lucky group too.

Most of us have to throw our own pebbles in the jar to bring the trickle of water to the top. I've wished for a big lottery-style win, a large stone that will overflow the jar in a beautiful waterfall, cascading over the sides, flooding the countertop where the jar sits. If you're like me, there's little chance of a waterfall overflowing the jar. If I wait for that to happen, the water of success will never reach the top of my jar. But if I add even just one tiny pebble at a time, eventually the water will spill over the top.

I can reach nearly any goal if I never give up, if I plod away, and if I add a pebble to the jar on a regular basis, no matter how small the pebble is. Running on the assumption that we are setting realistic goals for ourselves (we are assuming that my dream isn't to play professional basketball, as I'm under five feet two and I seriously lack the athleticism for that career—I'm also too old)., and that our dreams—even if big—are possible, the way to get there is to pebble. I've been a pebbler and I continue to pebble.

Regardless of how long it took me to arrive at the threshold of "professional writer" and "professional artist", I did eventually wake up one day and realize, "Wow, I did it!" Of course there can always be more money, and that's why I'm still a pebbler. I make a modest income—I won't oversell myself to you. Nonetheless, I have reached a level of success that exceeds the dreams I had for myself when I was a child. I wanted to "be a writer when I grow up" and indeed I am!

One day I'd like to pursue other dreams that I can't afford right now. I'd also like to be a philanthropist. My biggest dream in life is to be someone who can make a difference. Ah, but I can do that right now! Waiting for "when I am rich" or "when I'm a bigger celebrity" to make a difference is an excuse. There's no reason why I can't make a difference *today*. Besides, what if I never reach a higher level of success? No, there's no valid reason to wait for "someday". I've been through dark times and I've emerged on the other side. When I share what has worked for me, I might help someone else. I hope that I'll make a difference—that I'll make a difference for *you*.

Another thing that I've told my kids is that we all have a responsibility to use our talents and abilities to make this world a better place. I need to practice what I preach. Funny how these lectures always come back to bite me! When I look at my life honestly, what I've done thus far looks rather weak. I mainly write mysteries and thrillers, fiction. This seems like a trivial contribution to a hurting world. What more can I do? How can I make a difference?

I don't want to leave anything on the table. I want to be like a dry sponge when I die. I want every talent, every skill, and every ounce of my energy wrung out of me before I go. And I want to inspire others to do the same.

I'll begin by exploring the reasons why the world feels hateful. First of all, the world has *always* been hateful! Nothing we experience here on Earth is new. Someone has gone through something shockingly similar before, and nothing that happens to us ever shocks God. And this is where I may be losing some of you.

Religion brings out the haters in full force. For some, the word "God" causes ears to bleed, hearts to harden, and teeth to clench. I will explain my philosophy though because my advice comes from a faith-based perspective. As a reader, I like to know the philosophical viewpoint of an author before reading potentially life-changing advice by that person. I can then run it through my own filter and take in only that advice that fits into my own belief system.

I'll use an analogy to explain my personal faith (I'm fond of analogies, as you'll soon discover). I believe that the words "I do" in a wedding ceremony can either be pointless or deeply meaningful, depending on the person saying the vows. Some marriages end in divorce while others endure. Why do some people fall in love at first sight, while others fall in love with someone they didn't particularly like at first? How do some couples fall in love after an arranged marriage—with a person they have never even met?

I don't know. I don't know how love works, only that it does, and that it comes to people in different ways, and when people are in love, they know it. They are certain. They may even die so that the person they love will live.

I believe that God meets us "where we are". Like love, people who believe in God are certain. They just know. They may even die rather than deny their faith. Now, when I'm talking about God, I don't mean to honor any religion that hurts people, just as love should never be abusive. While religious beliefs may differ greatly from person to person, whenever religion is an excuse to hurt another person, it is hate. And that's another reason why I'm bringing this up. Religion is a trigger for haters.

All people have a religious belief, even if that belief is that there is no Higher Power. In an ideal world, all religions would be appreciated and supported to care for the needy and to make the world a better place. Instead of fighting over who is right and who is wrong, we'd agree upon one simple truth: love is right, hate is wrong. Ah, but we don't live in an ideal world.

I hate mentioning that I'm a Christian because I know that some of you cringe at the very sound of that word. If this is you, I'm sorry that you have had a negative association with a religion that is supposed to be about love. I too have been hurt by people who claim to be Christians. I've felt disrespected, misunderstood, and judged. Too many times I've tried to do something good and I was instead rejected because I was not Christian "enough" in their eyes. However, I'm also *loved* by Christians more deeply than by any other group of people, so please don't take my words to mean that I am condemning

Christians as a whole. I'm merely stating that I understand if you are wary, and I'm asking you to forgive people who have wronged you. If you let hateful people discourage you from becoming close to beautiful people, the haters win.

I've used Christianity as an example because it is the religion dear to my own heart, but we could make similar evaluations for all other religions. Religion is comprised of imperfect people who sometimes do horrible things in the name of religion. Don't believe them when they do this! A true religion advocates for love, not hate.

I am a person of faith even after people have failed me. Perhaps this is true of you as well. I believe that faith is like love. It just happens, and when it does, you are certain. No one can shake you from that certainty.

I also believe that God may come to you in a different way than He has come to me. My task is to love you, and that is all. If you've ever felt that people of faith are obnoxious,

I'm sorry. I know many religious people who are quiet, unassuming, and who would never tell anyone else what they should or should not believe. The voices you hear the most often are the voices that are the loudest. And maybe the noisy approach helps some people. I don't want to stand in their way. I only want to assure you that if you are inclined to view every religious person as a hater, do your best to let go of that perception. In my experience, few people will tell you what they believe unless you ask them. It's a shame that some of the most loving people of faith aren't noticed because they quietly respect your privacy, and because they modestly give generously to others without drawing attention to themselves. **Haters love attention.** Sadly, they overshadow the loving, kind, generous, and selfless people who can inspire others to believe that there is good in this world, if only their voices aren't drowned out by the finger-pointers.

13

Another thing I want to bring up: judging another person is expressly forbidden in the Bible, and in other religious texts as well, so do keep that in mind. People have taken it upon themselves to justify small mindedness. There's a bad apple in every barrel, but why should you toss out the whole barrel? While people who have a dysfunctional relationship with religion may well be haters, people of faith are not your enemy.

Religious people are a wonderful asset to this world (and to you personally) when they actively seek ways to love and serve others, especially when they join together as a group for charitable causes. So even if you've had a bad experience with religion or religious people, do your level best to keep an open mind. People of true faith are a treasure in a hateful world. There's no shortage of people who need help!

Back to the bad apples... not every religion is valid. I want to acknowledge that there's a difference between faith and the rules that men make up to explain it. God is about love, not hate, but people often twist religion until it resembles something ugly. Adding to the confusion is muddy history, ancient Scriptures that don't make sense, and sordid violent pasts that can't be shaken. Bottom line: Religion can be a trigger for hate. **If you are a person of faith, you might have a target on your back simply because you are religious.** I've had this happen to me. It's hard to be on the receiving end of venom coming from total strangers. When the hate mail began I hadn't even said much (yet) about religion. I think people may have been reacting to the cross necklace I wear in some of my author photos.

Politics is another obvious trigger. Religion and politics—it's a cliché by now that these two topics divide. I usually avoid talking about either, but I don't deny what I believe when asked, or when it makes sense to volunteer it (I'm an Independent voter, by the way). But every time I open my mouth, I can expect to attract haters. I don't drop inflammatory political statements into the pond for this reason, and I refrain from commenting when others do this. Why shake a hornet's nest? My advice is as old as the sun, but here goes: **Avoid talking about religion and politics.**

Having said this, good people speak up. Here's a tip for those times when you aren't sure if your urge to say something is courageous or, when viewed honestly, your contribution is just another rant from another angry person: Write or type your thoughts before saying or posting anything. Walk away. Wait at least five minutes before reading your words. Imagine that you hold the opposite point of view as yours. How do you feel as you read what you wrote? Are your words angry? Will your words change anyone's mind? If not, there's no purpose to contributing more anger into an already hateful world. Let it go. I can't tell you how many of my words I've deleted without sending! This method has saved me many times from conversations I would have regretted. Unfortunately I haven't always hit the delete key when I should have.

I do find that the practice of deleting without sending has become easier over time. When I'm in a cranky or sulky mood I delete more posts than I send! I also let my calls slide directly into voicemail. Trust me, it's better not to say anything at all than to say something that you can't take back. When you can't trust yourself, give yourself a time out.

To some extent I can avoid a hotbed of haters by not participating in those controversial discussions. Haters are triggered by differences in religion, politics, culture, social class, race, and gender---the very topics that matter to a healthy society. I don't like the idea that I'm allowing myself to be bullied into silence, so I try to recognize when I'm opting out because I'm a coward, as opposed to opting out because I'm wise. Being afraid to speak up is unacceptable, then again wisely holding my tongue is sometimes the best path.

My son had this enlightened comment about why people participate in angry debates, "Some people are addicted to the power of making other people feel uncomfortable." He was thirteen or fourteen years old at the time. If a child can see through the motives of haters, why can't we adults? Learn to recognize a conversation that will likely end up in a hot mess. Walk away!

Having said this, avoidance only works for the sparks we anticipate. Even if I'm wisely soft-spoken, I can't possibly avoid every trigger that sets haters off. Haters hate for trivial, bizarre, and often *ridiculous* reasons. Sometimes people hate us for **no reason at all**. We can't control what other people do, so it's best to move on from trying to figure this out. "Why" haters hate is a short conversation because this book is focused on how we can thrive regardless of being hated.

No matter who has hurt me, or why, the effect is that I feel unloved when it happens. I feel insignificant. I feel invisible. I feel like I don't matter. Oh, yes, I know that those three things mean essentially the same thing, but my heart wants to count every offense, even if the difference between two nearly identical slights is barely perceptible. I feel rejected. I feel disowned. I feel that I wasn't accepted in the first place. I feel forgotten. I feel lost. I feel broken.

But nothing stays broken that can be fixed, so my husband says. I've been married to Brent for over twenty-five years. No, this doesn't mean that I'm an elderly woman. I was a child bride of eighteen. Brent was nineteen and a Private in the United States Army. He received orders for a tour in Germany, so we decided to throw a quick wedding together ("we" meaning me of course).

During my freshman year of college, I had two months to schedule a traditional church wedding, a reception hall with a dance floor, a deejay, and a full-course dinner. I also arranged for my grandpa to fly in from New York to Indiana to walk me down the aisle; my dad had died from cancer two years earlier. It was a tall order, but I managed to pull off every detail, right down to the selection of perfect invitations, flowers, cake, and a beaded princess wedding dress with a train that extended for miles.

On the eve of the big day my fiancé was detained at the eleventh hour and almost missed our wedding. A snowstorm hit, delaying our wedding photographer. The wedding candle wasn't pre-lit and the pastor interrupted the service to ask if anyone in the church had "a light". It was an awkward moment of both embarrassment and heroism for the smokers in attendance to rise to the occasion and save the ceremony from dead air.

Our wedding was a comedy of errors, but nothing was broken that couldn't be fixed. I joined my new husband in Germany as planned, at the end of my college semester. We lived in the village of Geisfeld near the city of Bamberg for the first three years of our marriage.

Brent served on border patrol during the historic "fall of the wall". At the end of his tour he deployed to the Gulf War. When Desert Storm ended, he got out of the Army and we returned to the United States for more adventures: finishing college, getting a job, starting a family, and moving many, many times.

Our most recent move was a short one. We moved only about sixty miles away from our previous home, which made the experience much easier than most of our previous moves. Relocating is familiar territory by now and I have developed an efficiency that I'm proud of. My marriage in general has also become familiar territory. Our conversations repeat themselves so often that our kids can mouth the words we're about to say.

Me: "You broke it!"

Him: "No, I didn't. I can fix it."

Me: "But if you didn't break it, it wouldn't need to be fixed."

Him: "If I can fix it, it's not broken."

Me: "But you won't get to it. It's broken."

Him: "I'll get to it."

Me: "Can you just say you're sorry for breaking it?"

Him: "I can fix it."

The conversation generally fizzles out at that point. The rest of the pattern goes like this: Next, I add the broken item to his pile. Then the pile sits, and grows. Every now and then he takes an afternoon out of his life to repair the pile of broken things. Some of the items need glue, some need screws, and some need to be re-built. Some end up in the trash.

A couple of weeks ago we had a conversation, meaning that I delivered a monologue while he may or may not have listened. I told him that sometimes I need to hear him say that he is sorry when he does things that hurt me. My words were cluttered by a million other rambling thoughts that tumbled out of my mouth. I didn't know if any of it landed, and it wouldn't have mattered anyway. I wasn't going anywhere.

A few weeks ago Brent had the urge to seal a dripping skylight window with plastic sheeting. He was in our bedroom on an extension ladder, the soles of his slippers bent over the metal rails. I fussed about his safety. He told me not to watch. I'm not sure why we bother to repeat these conversations. By now we should be able to replay them telepathically.

I didn't watch him while he used scissors to cut the plastic sheeting to fit the window. But naturally I had re-entered the room at the precise moment when he was finished cutting the plastic and he dropped the scissors to the floor. The scissors hit the floor, bounced off of the carpet, and hit my stringed mountain dulcimer in its position on the wooden stand that my husband made me for Christmas. I gasped. I picked up the instrument and examined it. My heart sank when I saw that a chunk (well, more like a sliver) was missing from the beautiful wood.

Me: "You broke it."

Him: "No, really?"

Me: "It's OK. It's not that noticeable. At least it's not on the front. I can pretend it's not there."

[silence]

He inspects it. "Aw, I see it."

[silence]

Him: "I'm sorry."

Me: "I'm sad, but I'll get over it."

[silence]

Me: "Thank you."

[silence]

Him: "I can fix it."

And that sums up our marriage. Nothing between us is ever broken—we can fix it. I'd like to extend that analogy to everything else in life. Nothing is broken if we can fix it. Nothing hurts forever. We can dig deeper. We can fight to overcome. We can seek healing. We can survive anything the world throws at us.

If you're like me, you might be skimming this book for enlightenment, with no real intention of doing any homework. May I suggest that you'll benefit more if you work alongside me? Listening to my own experiences has limited benefit. Digging into *your own stuff* will help you much more. That's why I suggest that you write in a journal while reading this book. Now if the idea of putting pen and paper into use is beyond realistic expectations, why not write e-mails to yourself? It's a quick and easy way to get the job done. Yes, you can skim this book and still get something out of it, but don't you want healing and success? I'm guessing that's why you've chosen to read a book called "Thriving in a Hateful World".

So I challenge you to journal along with me. I'll help you discover what makes you tick and how to motivate yourself to keep adding pebbles to the jar. Stop hoping for that lottery win, for that waterfall to overflow the jar instantly, as you'll likely be wasting precious time waiting for something that will never happen. Read on, and commit yourself to thriving. Not only will I inspire you to put pebbles in your jar, but I will inspire you to put pebbles in your neighbors' jars! I'll encourage you to have patience to plod along for as long as it takes, while feeling hopeful, expectant, and loved.

Will you accept my challenge? I'm asking you to open your heart and your mind to a new way of looking at your life. The purpose of this book is to coach you to be at peace with "however long it takes" to fill your jar with pebbles. May you enjoy the journey, even if the road leads you to surprising places, and may you thrive in a hateful world!

2

ICE CREAM IN A CONE

My father was in the Air Force when I was a young child. We moved away from upstate New York but we always made at least one visit home per year. One of those going-home summers I was at Grandma and Grandpa's little blue house on the hill. The house was chock full of relatives, including over a dozen kids. When we heard the ice cream truck's music from the next block over, my cousins and I raced to the street, as our parents had promised us that we could each have an ice cream cone.

Seconds later I stood waiting in line by the truck. The heat of the sun seared through my fair skin, yet I did not leave my post. I watched one happy child after another skip away with ice cream in hand. I waited patiently until every one of my cousins was served. It didn't bother me to be last. I prided myself on being graceful about such things, not that anyone noticed. Finally it was my turn. I held my glorious straight-off-the-truck cone in my hands. I crossed the street and almost made it into my grandparents' driveway when disaster struck. My ice cream slid entirely off the cone and fell onto the street! I bit back the tears, as bravery under such circumstances was required. I said nothing and marched onward toward the house.

My uncle was astonished, I assume because I had immediately resigned myself to going without ice cream. "We'll get you another one, Natalie!" He led me back to the ice cream truck and bought me another cone. I didn't know what to say. It had been my fault. I had been careless. He was paying twice for something he should have been willing to pay for only once.

I wish I could say that my little girl self realized that I was worth a second chance. I also wish that I had learned that passively hanging back in the hot sun to let others go ahead in line was not heroic, but was instead needless suffering. No, I didn't get that message.

I missed the point entirely. I learned that my uncle was my favorite uncle! After all, he was nice to me even after I had made a mistake! Who else would be that nice? Who indeed? Well, hopefully the answer to that question going forward will always be—*me!* I will be nice to me!

Let's use my ice cream cone story to get us to the focus of Chapter Two. How can we thrive in a hateful world if we hate ourselves? What a horrible disadvantage we'll have if we're our own worst hater!

First, we'll examine the characters in my ice cream cone story. We'll begin with my parents. Now, this book isn't about judging my parents, but we won't make much progress if this book isn't honest. My parents, for reasons that don't matter right now, were harsh with me. For the purpose of this story, we'll simply say that I believed that my parents wouldn't have bought me a second cone. My mother was embarrassed that I had caused her brother to purchase a replacement cone, as she disliked it when I was a bother.

I'm forty-four years old now and I'm fully responsible for my own emotions. My parents are both deceased. If I choose to judge myself as harshly as they judged me, I have no one to blame but myself. Will I stand in harsh judgment over myself and be my own worst hater? Or will I forgive myself when I make mistakes? I'm worthy of a second ice cream cone! Unfortunately it has taken me nearly a lifetime to understand this.

My intention in sharing my ice cream story is not to encourage you to identify people who have hurt you, and to then hold a grudge against that person(s). No! My purpose in sharing this story is to illustrate how we judge ourselves through the same eyes that someone else has judged us. No one but God has the authority to judge us, but this doesn't get us off the hook. If you have wronged someone, fix it and move on. If you are innocent of wrong doing, then drop your self-condemnation right now. Give yourself a new ice cream cone.

Forgive yourself for your human moments. Someone once told me that low self-esteem is the biggest form of vanity. The reasoning behind this is that only a person who is self-absorbed will look inward with the devotion and scrutiny required to judge oneself. People who are focused on other people's needs are too busy to be narcissistic.

They are too generous to be selfish. Thoughtful and giving people don't have low self-esteem.

This line of thinking has both helped and harmed me. When I've been in a funk I've been able to give myself a swift kick in the pants by reminding myself that wallowing is selfish. However, I've also allowed this line of thinking to condemn me for feeling worthless. I caution you to take the "low self-esteem is selfish" concept with a grain of salt. Use it if it motivates you, but drop it if you become your own worst hater. I think the core advice is more valuable after minor tweaking: "An effective way to boost your self-esteem is to focus on others."

Make a difference for someone else in a positive way. Positive energy begets positive energy. On the other hand, some of us with low self-esteem fall into the trap of focusing on others to the point of dysfunctional enabling. We allow ourselves to disappear. There's no cookie-cutter fix for how to fire yourself as your own worst hater. It's a process.

So, not knowing who you are, or where you are at this point in your life, I'll conclude that your reaction to judgment is something only you can determine. If you've done something wrong—fix it and forgive yourself. If you haven't done anything that needs to be fixed, consider the possibility that you are spending too much time focused on yourself, but don't add "I'm selfish" to the list of things to condemn yourself for! "Don't wallow" is something you can tell yourself if you're looking inward too much. No matter what you've done, or haven't done, God loves you. And who knows better than God? Don't let anyone tear down what God made—*you.*

Next I'll look at the role my uncle played. He extended grace to me by giving me a second cone even though I had dropped the first one. How can I be that person for someone else? How can I extend grace to others, starting with my own children?

Ah, but I'm getting ahead of myself. Before we can move forward to thrive in a hateful world, we have to clear the air. Do we hate ourselves? Are we holding ourselves back? Do you need to make amends for something? The past might be haunting you. Make a list of the first five stories from your childhood that pop into your head. Chances are, you have your own ice cream in a cone story.

My story has a happy ending, at least as far as my career as an oil painter and author is concerned. Two recent articles about my artistic career summarize this nicely. I hope that my journey encourages you to pursue your own dreams (or stick with what you're doing if you're already well on your way), no matter how many people tear you down.

As published by The Alliance of Independent Authors blog, October 2013:

My Journey as an Artist

~

"When I was a little girl I would draw pictures and people would gather around to watch me. My family said that I inherited my father's artistic talent. But when I went to elementary school, my art teacher thought otherwise. She said, 'There's no special way you have to do it'. My heart sang! I had permission to do the project as I wished, and I did. I was confused and heartbroken when she held my art project up for the entire class to see. 'Don't do yours like Natalie has done.'

I was a shy child and I was humiliated into silence. Every week I'd try again, and most of the time I got the same unfortunate result: my teacher was disgusted. It didn't take long before I believed that no one 'important' would ever like what I did. In high school, I finally had a wonderful nurturing art teacher and my confidence soared. I learned new skills and I took more and more art classes. I entered the school's career art program. I also painted theater sets for the drama department. I went to college feeling as if I could major in art.

I thought wrong. My college professors were as disappointed with me as my elementary school teacher had been. What made the experience worse was that each professor encouraged student critiques. The professors' personal bias about my work colored the sessions, as one student after another strived to critique my work in a more verbose way than the student before had done, in a competition to condemn my work in the most arrogant and harsh language they could conjure up. After a semester of soul-trashing and mob-critiquing, one of my professors looked me in the eyes and said that people like me are not artists.

I quit. I never painted another picture again. That is, I never painted again until my husband surprised me with a beautiful freestanding easel for Christmas. I was speechless, and conflicted. It had been at least twenty years since I'd done any real art. Sure, I'd dabbled. I painted nursery themes on the kids' walls and I taught a few art classes here and there, but I hadn't done anything serious enough to justify having a professional artist's easel. There were wheels on it! It was expensive. What was my husband thinking?

But the look on his face! He had even put a bright red bow on it. How could I disappoint him? Surely I could paint one painting. I tried oil paints for the first time in my life and I loved it! I painted one painting after another. Then I saw an advertisement for a call to artists. I decided to enter one of my paintings. I was accepted! It didn't pay anything, but my hopes were high. However, several years passed and I couldn't sell my paintings, not even at a garage sale. As people walked past my original oil paintings without even a passing glance, I felt silly for even trying. I threw my paintings in the trash bin when the garage sale was over.

My son dug my paintings back out of the trash and hung them on the wall in our house. I promised never to throw my paintings away again. But my career as an artist was obviously going nowhere. Unless I didn't mind painting as a hobby, there was no point in continuing. I focused on my writing career, once again feeling that I was never going to be a professional artist.

My easel came back out of storage when I needed original artwork for my mystery series. Because I'm an indie author I have the freedom to choose my own cover artist - I chose me. I considered it a simple errand to meet a need. I never dreamed that it would be the beginning of a career as an oil painter! I created a Kickstarter project to fund the oil paints and canvas. I figured that if I raised funds for the project it was worth doing, and if I failed to raise support I'd put a cover together using random stock photography. I was funded, but more importantly I was encouraged.

One thing led to another, and now my paintings are in galleries and exhibits. I divide my time between writing and painting as I have steady work in both careers. I'll even need to set up a second easel because I have two art project deadlines that overlap! My current projects include a Doctor Who themed oil painting for a charity auction at the Doctor Who convention in Minneapolis, and a fantasy landscape painting for a gallery exhibit.

It made all the difference when my family believed in me, even when others did not. It also helped when teachers believed in me, and when my Kickstarter project was funded. But the most important of all is that I finally believed in myself. It took me a long time to be discovered as an artist and I did quit more than once. I now know that I was born to paint: I no longer need anyone's permission to be an artist, and today when my paintings are held up for everyone to critique, they are held up high - on a gallery wall!"

~

A similar article about my journey as an author was published only twenty-four hours apart from the article about my art career! The timing of the publication of these two articles was serendipitous, as the plans for these articles were on two completely different timetables (months in the making) and were from separate sources (with different reasons for each topic). This remarkable coincidence encouraged me. When the articles came out I had been wavering in confidence about a new project.

When unrelated events align themselves I take notice. Randomness on its own doesn't help me, but my reaction to it matters. After seeing my own words in these two articles side-by-side, I realized that my author journey and my artist journey were more related than I had been aware of—namely, I realized that one of the main barriers to my success was my lack of confidence. In reference to the good witch Glinda from *The Wizard of Oz*, I had the power in me all along. After this message hit home, I was motivated to live up to my own press! I took on the project that I had been considering. It opened new doors for me, doors that would have remained closed if I hadn't stepped out in confidence to try something new.

As published by Shelf Help at BenGalley.com, October 2013:

My Journey as an Author

~

"At the beginning of my career I didn't think much about how a writer becomes a novelist. I thought the important part was writing a book, so I did. Then I researched how to find a publisher and a literary agent. I wrote another book. Then I wrote two more books. During this time I was regularly receiving rejection slips. One of my favorites said 'Authorgram' at the top, with a check box below for the editor to select 'does not suit our present needs'. Another slip said, 'Dear ____' The editor didn't bother to fill in the blank with my name.

Eventually I did receive an acceptance for one of my manuscripts. I was elated! I wondered when my book would be in libraries. My elation dampened when the publisher said that I was accepted but "on hold". I was on hold for two years. I followed up, I inquired, I nagged. Eventually I asked if I should be looking elsewhere. I was told that I was free to explore my options.

My husband then suggested that I publish the books myself. This was 1997. There was no such animal as indie publishing then. Self-publishing was called vanity publishing. I was mortified. Apparently my husband didn't think I was publishable! No, he clarified, he meant that I was letting people stop me from being a published author. I had studied marketing in college, I was computer savvy, and I was a sharp cookie. Why was I still waiting? Why, indeed!

My self-publishing journey began with reading books by John Kremer and Dan Poynter. The Internet was still a fuzzy arena where only nerds like me gathered. Book marketing and publishing was a real-world brick and mortar experience with a huge boys' club network. Because this was a world that was closed to indies, the experts recommended creating an imprint to publish under. And so it was that I was sitting all by myself at the Independent Spirit Publishing table at a trade show in Saint Paul, Minnesota 1999.

To put this in perspective for you, I was the only self publisher there. Everyone else was a representative, a guest author, or a publisher from presses small, mid-sized or mammoth. Most were attending with an entire team of people. No one else was alone from what I recall. Some displayed their authors' many titles on freestanding revolving racks. Tables were decked out with commercial displays, glossy marketing materials, freebies, catalogs and premiums.

My table, on the other hand, was covered with a fabric tablecloth from home. I decorated my table in a pizzeria theme to showcase my 'pizza detective' series, an improvisation because I had no commercial displayers. I was in my twenties at the time, and I looked even younger. How I managed to attract any attention at all is beyond me, but I did. A publisher at the trade show took an interest in my series.

That interest led to hopefulness that I would be published 'for real'! Unfortunately the expectations for travel exceeded what I was willing to do. I had small children at the time and I didn't want to commit to 'at least fifty book signings' a year. The commitment was nonnegotiable, I tried. At that point, I realized that the quest for publication had become frustrating beyond what I could handle. I was out of money, out of patience and out of time. I took a long break from writing books and diverted my attention elsewhere. I wrote scripts for community theater and local indie movies. I contributed to other people's books. I wrote magazine articles. I wrote a newspaper column.

I was a writer, but I didn't feel like an author anymore. I was also weary of storing the boxes and boxes of books that I couldn't sell. This was before the technology of print on demand. I had used a credit card to finance standard small print runs of my books from a commercial printer. I'd made some sales, and a few libraries even bought my books, but the cheap quality of the low-end printing option- the only option I could afford- was disappointing. I was done with the whole experience. How silly and vain of me to store these 'vanity' books!

I then spent three days burning my books in a giant bonfire in our backyard. As I stared at the fiery pages, the air lifted them up and up, dancing and swirling. The ashes eventually fell down, down, down the hill to the house across the road. I saw my neighbor pick up one of my charred pages and read it. I ignored that embarrassment, and plowed through. Then I accidentally burned myself. My humiliation was complete; I looked like I had a bad sunburn on my chest for weeks and my books that had failed to burn completely were making a mess of our property. Every time I saw a page sticking out of the grass I felt mocked.

Years later, my kids grew. The theater and dance business I was directing ended. I became my terminal mother's caregiver. The recession in America was in full swing. I had a sensation that life was passing me by. Why was I sitting on my dreams? It was time to attack my goals with everything I had. Surely by now I had grown as a person and as a writer. I wasn't the twenty-something girl sitting behind a tablecloth. I was in my forties now and a little thing called e-Books had created a gold rush.

I wrote another book, *Angels Mark*. It hit Amazon's bestseller list after a successful free book promotion. I received the best paycheck I had ever had in all of my years as a working writer combined! The next two years were a flurry of promotion, writing, publishing, and surprises. I wrote five more books and launched into unexpected new careers. Painting the book covers for my books brought attention to my skills as an oil painter. I have since had several of my paintings on exhibit in galleries and shows. Painting gives me great joy and peace. I never would have thought that I'd have the opportunity to be a working artist. Another career tangent is in comedy. My public speaking workshops for libraries has led to comedic topics. I have always enjoyed making people laugh and clowning at the microphone. I was a big cheese at the last high school reunion I attended. I never expected that I would have the opportunity to be a professional comedienne. I could go on with this subject for quite a stretch: my indie publishing career has allowed me to be an entrepreneur, living my dreams.

When I first started this journey, I needed to be shameless and creative with my marketing efforts. I met then-Governor of Minnesota Jesse Ventura and signed a book for his wife. I received a mention on his official website, my fifteen minutes of fame as the press snapped pictures and the cameras rolled, and the story of it appeared in the book 'Confessions of Shameless Self Promoters'. Fast forward to now: I still do crazy things to promote my books, but the effects of my promotions are immediate and amazing! I can use QR codes to direct people to my books. I can give people free-to-produce samples of my work, instantly!

My moxie and spirit from 1998 has no boundaries in 2013. The bad news? 'Everyone' can write a book. The good news? There's only one me. My fan base continues to grow. And guess what? My books are now in hardcover editions on library shelves! My journey was a long and windy road, and I've been indie when indie wasn't cool. I was close to giving up when I literally burned my books in a fire, but the desire to be an author couldn't be destroyed that easily. I'm grateful for this new world of publishing where there is room at the table for every author who is willing to pull up a chair and get to work."

~

What's your own story? How did you get where you are today? Pay attention to what your stories reveal about what has hurt you along the way. Conquer the past, heal the present, and thrive in the future.

Forgive others, forgive yourself, and move on. If you need help doing this, please consider seeking therapy from a reputable source. I'm assuming that you are in a good place mentally, spiritually, and emotionally, and that you are open to making changes.

Take an honest look at yourself. Search your heart. Are you ready for Chapter Three, or do you need a time out to address old hurts?

NATALIE BUSKE THOMAS

3

SOCKS IN A DRAWER

Sometimes we've done all we can to forgive and to let go, but our losses remain. How long do we grieve for a loved one who has passed away? How long do we grieve a miscarriage, a stillbirth, or the death of a child? How long will our grief hold us back from thriving?

In Chapter Two I was outspoken about letting go of past hurts, but I wasn't talking about grief. I was talking about negative experiences that might lead to self-doubt or resentment. Grief is entirely different, and advising you to let go of that kind of hurt may be the worst advice I can give you.

There are some losses that never go away, and we might not want them to. The weight on our soul is almost welcome; because it keeps us connected to the people we have lost. Our pain is forever a part of who we are, and for many of us, we wouldn't have it any other way.

Ignore all of those friends who urge you to move on, especially since their motivation for rushing you through your grief is likely due to their own discomfort instead of looking out for your best interests. Do you want to move on? You may not be ready. You may never be completely ready. Our loved ones are far enough from us. Why would we push them away? No, I need to clarify that pain from grief is a different type of hurt. We can heal from loss while also holding the pain close to our hearts, in a way that still allows us to move on to a healthy new life. We can move on from the darkness while still holding on to the love. There is peace in sadness, and if you aren't ready to let go, don't give in to the pressure to do so.

When my mother was dying I read several self-help books. I'm not sure what I was looking for exactly, but if I had to name what it was, I'd call it "empathy". People who had expressed *sympathy* for my situation felt sorry for me, but they often didn't know what to say. People who had expressed *empathy* for me had firsthand experience with grief and were more likely to say something comforting. I wanted to be understood. I wanted reassurance that the hole in my heart wouldn't hurt forever, even though I knew that it wouldn't. All the same, I wanted to be told what I already knew. I wanted to be told what I already knew many times over. I wanted to hear this truth every time I felt my loss, which was often.

I found it easier to withdraw from family and friends than to pretend that I was feeling fine. I wasn't feeling fine, and I wouldn't be quite the same ever again. That's what grief does to a person, and I know this all too well.

I had been through many losses before losing my mom. I knew that the spiritual process of healing eventually brings us all to the point where the hurt isn't sharp anymore and a new normal begins, even if we are dragging our feet through the transition. One day there's a spontaneous moment of joy, and then another. A baby is born into the family, a career change or relocation initiates a new lifestyle, people get married, rainbows grace the sky. Life goes on.

And if it doesn't? If your sadness is not a peaceful bittersweet remembrance, but instead your loss lingers as a dark and exhausting depression, please do seek help. I'm not a therapist and I don't want any of you harmed by my book. Everything I'm telling you is based on my own personal experiences—you might be in a different situation. Listen to your family and friends if they are urging you to seek help.

Assuming that you are healing on a rather predictable schedule, the grief does fade. *Eventually* it does. And even though I know this to be true, when I'm hurting, I need to hear that I'll be O.K., that I'll make it through to the other side of this. If you are in this situation, please listen: you'll be OK. Hold on—look for comfort and you will find it. Do what you need to do to pass the time until your season of grief fades.

5 Tips to Help You Grieve

1) Listen to hauntingly beautiful music at bedtime, and any time when you need a good cry.

2) Talk to someone who reminds you that you'll feel better eventually—that no season lasts forever, but who also understands that you do not feel good *today*. Books, audio books, television, and the Internet can all help. Make sure that you use only trustworthy resources.

3) Eat well, sleep well, and take good care of yourself overall. These familiar rituals of self-care can be done slowly and gently, as if you are a baby and someone else is taking care of you. Light candles, play music, take a long shower or a slow bubble bath. Wear soft fabrics and nice

clothes. Pay attention to your own skin. What do you see in the mirror? You need to make sure that you don't get sick. Resist self-medicating with drugs, alcohol or any escapism. Give yourself permission to *feel* your pain and gently help yourself through.

4) Pay it forward. Think now about how you might do that. You can be there for someone else. You can volunteer in your community in a way that feels connected to your grieving experience.

5) Find something good. What can you do with your life to make sense of your grief? Tragic events feel so heartbreakingly random and unjust. How can you make something positive come of this? How can you give meaning to the suffering? Is there anything you haven't done that you always wanted to do? Is there something you've been holding back on? Pledge now

to live fully! Give honor to your loved one and to your grief by channeling your loss into living your best life. Refuse to take senseless loss as the final answer. Give meaning to what has happened to you. Make a difference!

Those of us who have been through loss have stories about friends and relatives who behaved in shockingly inappropriate ways during or after the death experience. I've noticed that people who are most likely to behave in a hurtful way are those who feel uncomfortable with complicated emotions. Even a casual brush with someone who is grieving is enough to make them feel squeamish. It would be better for *them* if we would move on quickly, to save them from unpleasant feelings. Sometimes people who are intensely uncomfortable with death will even stir up controversy as a distraction from the real feelings of loss. When this happens, an entire family might become forever polarized over things that were said that can't be taken back.

Oftentimes, no one knows how the whole thing got started, as no one has an awareness of the root of the problem. People react differently to grief. One dysfunctional response can ensnare an entire family. It's helpful when an emotionally mature person provides leadership so that cooler heads prevail, and runs interference so that immediate family members have privacy.

I'm not excusing bad behavior. I'm merely offering an explanation. Sometimes it helps if we understand that the human condition is often the reason why people are predictable in disappointing ways. And on that note, people are predictable in another reaction as well. In nearly every crisis, people we barely know will come out of the woodwork to emerge as heroes. This phenomenon can feel healing and helpful, while also vaguely disturbing in a way that you might not be able to put your finger on. Not all help is welcome, especially if the offers to help come across as demanding and intrusive.

Having been down this road so many times, I've recognized that some of the people who rush to help me are "drama chasers". As soon as the rush of an emergency situation subsides, drama chasers drop me and move on to the next fix. This pattern is dysfunctional, and since the drama chaser often has little or no relationship with the person they are helping, the whole situation might feel awkward and invasive.

On the other hand, drama chasers are often wonderful people who are high-energy powerhouse personalities. They might be drama addicts, but they are also people who enjoy helping others in need, and can't turn down any situation in which they know they can lend a hand. I'm bringing this up because it took me a long time to understand why I had mixed feelings when near-strangers or even absolute strangers have jumped into my personal life. In some ways, I felt an invasion of privacy.

Not all Good Samaritans who rush to my aid are drama chasers. I know kindhearted people who have reached out to me in ways that matter. One friend leads a busy life and we didn't stay in touch regularly, but during two of my darkest hours she dropped by my home with food for my family. She offered a warm hug, and respectfully kept the visit short. It was the right touch, the right message, and deeply appreciated. I'm not talking about this kind of spontaneous gesture.

I think you probably know what I mean, about the difference between genuine offers of help and offers that seem "off". There's an overzealous quality and an overbearing demeanor in people who are drawn to a crisis. If I had to guess, I'd say that drama chasers have a compulsion. They need to feel needed. And all of this may be of benefit to you, or it might feel like you have a new stalker. My point in bringing this up is that loss can bring out bizarre behaviors in people, such as in the drama chaser example in which a person you barely know inserts themselves into your life when you are vulnerable. Loss also brings out haters.

I'm dedicating an entire chapter on loss for two reasons:

1) You might be coming from a place of loss that you need to heal from in order to thrive.

2) Loss can be a catalyst for hate. Sometimes hateful things are said when people are grieving. Grief may also become resentment, and motivate people to act hatefully for the rest of their lives.

If you are struggling through a loss, take your time and seek gentle healing to move through the process. Let go of unkind words that may have been said. Let go of any weirdness that may have left you feeling unhinged. Your grief journey is yours alone—don't let anyone interfere with it.

After losing my father, my cousin, my grandmother, and my uncle, I was a veteran of grief. So by the time my mom died, I had a better understanding of what I needed. I didn't let anyone rush me through the grieving process.

The grieving period is an extraordinary and sometimes magical time in which the hours and days are out of sync with the rest of the world. It is a time for privacy, reflection, and stillness. Moments are precious, fleeting, and will never return. While in our grief we have an awareness of the gift of time, but the Earth spins on its axis the same as always.

The rest of the world plods through their average days as if nothing has changed, as if a significant human being hadn't just left this planet. It's a cruel reality that life goes on. How predictable and trivial are the events of an ordinary day. People get caught up in the things that don't matter while missing the things that do.

But for the grieving, there is an acute awareness of how precious a single moment is. There is an understanding of how fleeting our days are, here on planet Earth. There is wisdom in knowing that all things die, and that one day we too will die. There is beauty in despair.

There are few times in our lives when we have a window, a glimpse, into the Light on the other side—when suddenly the meaning of life is clear. We know what we must do. We must live! We need to make each moment count. Everything matters. Oh why have we wasted so much time? There's much to do! We need to slow down and savor, and yet we need to speed up and live life faster.

If we allow grief to change us, we will transition into stronger and better human beings. That magical window in which the days stand frozen in time while the rest of the world marches on is short. Even if you want to slow down the clock, you cannot. One day you will realize with a bit of a shock that you have rejoined the world of marchers in an ordinary day.

Ready or not, normalcy does resume. And when it does, you'll forget most of what you intuitively knew without a shadow of a doubt. One day your thirst for living will fade. You'll go for longer and longer periods without thinking about death, and therefore you'll go for longer and longer periods without thinking about what it means to truly live.

When you are in a season of grief, allow the time to pass at its own pace. Let your heart hear every whisper. Let the rain fall on you. Refresh your stale spirit with this new awareness of life, of love, and of the person who has left this world. Let all of this change you in a powerful and lasting way. The greatest tribute we can give our loved ones is to use our grief to be better, to make a difference. Their spirit, their time on this Earth, can give you the energy you need to be the life force for the both of you.

Will you become closer to God during this time? If so, don't let Him go when life marches back into normalcy! Will you mourn for the intimacy you had with your lost loved one, now that the memorial service and the estate distractions are well behind you? Don't let go! Your loved one is as near to you as you want them to be.

Well, of course you want your loved one here with you in the flesh. But in your spirit, you once felt them close to you—remember how you felt during your grieving period? Maybe you saw something outside that, for a flicker of second, you just *knew* it was a sign. Maybe it was a bird that flew and hovered mysteriously in the window that you happened to be looking through at that very moment. Maybe it was a penny that you found on your seat on a plane—how did it get there? Maybe it was a letter that you found when sorting through old papers. Maybe it was a phrase that someone said, that meant something special between you and your loved one, the reminder of a conversation that only the two of you shared. Whatever it was, I feel confident that you did feel your loved one near you, even if for but a passing second. I want to encourage you to grab hold of those special connections, whether you felt them directly or whether you felt them through another person's accounts. The connection to your lost loved one transcends beyond this Earth. Your relationship with them is *yours to keep for the rest of your life, to heal and comfort you.*

But what if your relationship with the deceased was less than perfect? What if the relationship was far from perfect? The relationship is now on your terms! If you had a dysfunctional and hurtful relationship with the person you have lost, remember that their spirit has no power of you. What can I say to convince you that you are free? Please know that you are. Any bondage to the past is of your own making—Release yourself from that prison!

What I meant by "your relationship with them is yours to keep for the rest of your life" is that it is entirely *your choice* to maintain and nurture that spiritual connection, as a source of comfort and encouragement. Pay attention to what you see and hear.

A flower may open impossibly late in the season. Is this a sign from your loved one? I saw a single flower growing in rock, opening during the early winter, in Minnesota! I was sure that this flower, growing near the flower bed where I had cut flowers for Mom when I was her caregiver, meant something deeply personal and spiritual. Whether it really did or not, does it matter? I believed it, it gave me hope and peace, and it helped me get through the day.

I believe that God may send us these signs, and that it's perfectly fine with Him if we believe that these are messages from our loved ones. Maybe they are, maybe they aren't.

These spiritual connections are real when I experience them, and they help. I'm not interested in an explanation. I am grateful for the mystery.

Here's another event that is a common occurrence for many:

A song randomly plays in the grocery store at the precise moment when you are feeling sad, while you are staring at the brand of coffee you once shared with the person you lost. The music cuts through your brain fog and you recognize the familiar tune as a song that has special meaning for the pair of you. I believe that your loved one is saying, "I see you. I don't want you to be sad. Be well. Be happy. I love you." Music is frequently a healing source that transcends time and place.

These are the things you can grab hold of and cling to. Don't let anyone tell you that you have to "let go". You do *not* have to let go! You can hold on to whatever you want to. Let go of only those things that hurt you. Keep what helps. Keep what heals. Keep what comforts.

I have seen many rainbows in my lifetime and I've seen more double rainbows than anyone else I've ever met. I've been frequently told that after meeting me, people see double rainbows even if they had never seen one before. I doubt that I'm a magical person who rubs off on others. My theory is that I inspire people to *look*. Look for rainbows. Look for signs from above. What are you missing out on that could bring you comfort and joy?

Allow yourself to believe in the impossible, to have faith, to see beauty in despair, and to see life in death. And then *live your life in the best way possible*. Be a miracle for someone else. Be that light in the darkness. Reject negative people, avoid haters, and allow yourself to be loved, not only by the living, but by all people who have ever loved you. Love yourself.

Before moving on from this topic, let me revisit the situation of a complicated relationship. I don't think that people give enough attention to a less-than-perfect passing, and I don't want my rainbows and flowers to gloss over reality. Just because someone has died, it doesn't mean that that person was perfect when he/she was alive, and sometimes they leave behind unfinished business. You may feel uncomfortable when pressured by society to honor your loved one with a memorial that doesn't feel honest. You may even doubt that you have the right to grieve. Yet your loss may hit you much harder than you ever expected that it would. And while you remember the imperfect reality, you may agonize over the loss of the person you love.

You do not need to re-invent the truth to make it fit someone else's expectations. You are entitled to grieve for an imperfect person who lived in an imperfect world, grounded in reality. It's your life, and it's your truth. When a relationship is complicated, is your grief less meaningful than the grief that nearly-perfect families bear? No. Your grief story is yours alone. Don't let anyone define it for you.

Imperfect people love us. And when they die, we grieve for them. We may not want everything back as it was, but we mourn the loss of the person we loved. Don't let anyone diminish your love and grief by criticizing you if you are honest about having conflicting emotions. You don't have to justify yourself to anyone. It is not necessary to pretend that the relationship you had with the deceased was better than it really was. However, some people have a hard time with this concept. When someone dies, people often take the position that negative realities are to be denied.

If you feel the need to unburden your heart of past hurts, make sure that you choose only safe people to share your thoughts with. Find people who unconditionally support you, who know you well, but who are *not related to the loved one*. Consider seeing a professional counselor if you need more help, especially if you can't find a listening ear who didn't have a personal relationship with the deceased.

Avoid drudging up past hurts with other family members. This can be perceived as disrespecting the loved one's memory. Respect that not everyone will acknowledge your truth, and that your truth may damage others. Some people may never believe your experience and may forever believe in a different reality. Let go, and accept your differences. If a family member refuses to hear anything less than glowing praise about your loved one, respect that and move on.

But maybe you aren't struggling to hold your thoughts back. Maybe you have the opposite problem: Do you want to pretend that nothing was ever bad between you and your loved one? Hold fast to the truth of the relationship with the person you lost, and cherish what was good. You don't need to ignore the truth to do that—your negative experiences will never nullify love. We can only do our best with what we've been given, and facing up to reality allows us to heal and move on. You aren't a bad person because you have loved an imperfect person. None of us are perfect! Accept what was, and focus on the love between the two of you.

To be clear, I'm not talking about relationships that are estranged. Estrangement is a different situation altogether. In the case of estrangement, death may come as a relief, especially if the person who died was dangerous. A "complicated" relationship is a less-than-perfect relationship that is a confusing jumble of good times and bad, whereas an estranged relationship may not be confusing at all. Dismiss any guilt you may be holding on to. Allow yourself to move on.

Love covers all wrongs, but the truth is still important. Ignore haters who tear you down if you confess that your relationship with the person you lost was complicated or even estranged. Even better, don't bare your soul to people who don't support you. Not everyone needs to know your personal truth; allow yourself to let go of the idea that everyone will understand you. Haters hate. Some people blame the victim for reasons that are unfathomable.

What I want to impress upon you most of all is that "complicated" doesn't mean invalid. When you lose someone you love, you deserve a grieving period that heals and comforts you on your terms. There are no rules about what your relationship had to be. Hold fast to the good. If your loved one was hard to love, consider how much harder you both had to work; be proud of the positive connections. Honor the truth, but don't keep score. Be grateful for the good in what you had.

I want to share with you my story *Christmas Socks*. It was featured on ReadWave and it solicited dozens of comments from people who could relate to it. As a side note, when I signed online to get this story just now, there was a message from ReadWave in my inbox, informing me that my story was selected for inclusion in a permanent collection called "loss". I'll take this remarkable coincidence in timing as confirmation that I should include *Christmas Socks* in this book.

Christmas Socks

*For a season I gave her something to live for while
my own life faded from view*

When my mother was terminally ill every
meal was a death-row last request. She wanted
potatoes fried in bacon grease, a specific brand
of chips, meatball sandwiches, and sausages
that were shipped to us, near Minneapolis,
from her hometown in upstate New York. I
couldn't fix what was broken in our lives and I
couldn't change what was going to happen, but
I could make her fried potatoes--as many times
as she wanted them. I could race around the
grocery store looking for the brand of chips
she wanted. These things were what we lived
for.

For a season I gave her something to live
for while my own life faded from view. One
day while changing Mom's oxygen hose she

suddenly looked up at me wide-eyed and said, "His voice changed." We looked at my son, who seemed at that moment to have grown up overnight. While chasing down the bag of chips for Mom I had missed my little boy. I looked at my two daughters. They too had grown. These were different kids from when this all started.

We were entangled, Mom and I. She requested music, all the songs from the old days. She talked about people she used to know. She talked about people who had died. She talked about things she wanted to do; things I knew would never happen. Together we looked through her treasures. She had stockpiled more than a lifetime of rubber bands, packaging tape, and paper. She had a box full of things that had never been opened. I saw a few of the gifts I'd given her over the years, never used.

After she died I cleaned out her apartment. In her dresser drawer was not one, but two pairs of fuzzy Christmas socks that I put in her stocking years ago. I remembered how her eyes had lit up when she saw the socks. The socks were still bound together with their holiday ribbon and the tag was still fixed. I gave the socks to my girls. I told them that they were to wear them, and they happily complied.

I think of those Christmas socks as I found them in her drawer, never used. The sight of them with their ribbons and tags still haunts me. I vowed that I will never save my fuzzy Christmas socks. I'll wear them even if it's July. I'll wear them even with sandals. I'll even give them away to someone else. But you'll never find my socks tucked away in a drawer with the ribbons and tags on.

4

THIS WORLD IS NOT MY HOME

Are you a Christian? Are you Jewish? Do you have any religious belief or spiritual faith that sets you apart from the world? If so, you already know all too well that this world is not your home. Darkness hates Light. Evil hates Love. If you are a person who loves and serve others, you are probably hated. If you dare to also love a Higher Power, giving God—not man, not government—your allegiance, you are doubly hated.

Are you an independent thinker? Do you speak your mind about politics, new ideas, and educational concepts? If you love philosophy and innovation, you are likely hated. The world despises those who seek to enlighten and change. Independent thinkers are difficult to control. Haters like power.

Are you an activist? Do you seek to make the world a better place? Do you most of all desire that people be free to live as they wish? Haters fear those who help the oppressed become free. Bullies don't like to see their victims empowered.

Chances are that you are a person of faith, an independent thinker, an activist, or all three. Maybe you are hated for the color of your skin, your gender, your disability, or something else that you can't quite put your finger on, but we all have this in common: Haters fear us because we are different.

Haters prefer people who are all the same, people who do not answer to a High Power, people who do not think for themselves, and people who do not stand up for others. In short, haters want to control you. If you are not easy to control, they will break you down until you are. Don't let them!

In Section One, I talked about areas where you might not be ready to thrive. If you haven't let go of past hurts or if you are in the grieving process, you might need to work on those issues before taking on the world. Go easy on yourself and recognize if you need a time out. Heal, let go, and then return to this book when you are ready. However, if you've sailed through Section One and you've determined that you are ready to thrive, you need to first identify and understand the enemy. You chose to read this book for a reason. I assume that you believe that the world is a hateful place. Let's get to the reasons why the world feels hateful. When we can name our enemies we can conquer them. Denial and sugar-coating have no business in this book. If you want to make real changes you have to begin with honesty.

Who hates you and why? Are you doing anything to encourage haters? I've been through rough patches when I was feeling victimized from all directions. I wondered if there was anything I was doing wrong. Is *everyone* hated? Or is this happening to just me—is this my fault? The answer that I came up with is yes, and yes. Yes, everyone is hated from time to time. And yes, it is (partially) my fault, as in, there are steps I can take to minimize the problem.

Here is a tip that has helped me: **Don't argue with invisible people!** Avoid passive aggressive behavior with these 4 rules about venting.

Don't Vent

1) When you're angry with a stranger

Examples: You're mad when a crying baby has spoiled your event—why didn't the parent leave when the child was inconsolable? You're mad when a driver is on the phone and he/she cuts you off in traffic. You're mad when you buy a product and it's obvious that someone had purchased that product before you did, and had returned it to the store with missing parts.

2) When you're angry with an organization, institution, or business

Examples: You're mad about new government regulations. You're mad about a decision the school district made. You're mad about something the church has done. You're mad about the customer return policy at a retail store. You're mad about the garbage pickup schedule in your city.

You're mad about a cancelled appointment from your dentist office.

3) When you're angry with someone you know

Examples: You're mad at your neighbor because he's burning leaves in his yard again. You're mad at your co-worker because he ate your yogurt. You're mad at your friend because she cancelled plans at the last minute, or because she showed up with a child who has a hacking cough and a runny nose.

4) When you're angry with someone close to you

Example: You are mad at your spouse, child, friend, or relative about something personal.

I've broken the above rules when I was angry with one person or organization, but I vented my frustration onto an innocent party. I add more anger to an already hateful world when I do this. And most of the time no one can help me with my problem anyway! What generally happens is that some of my listeners will then jump in with similar rants of their own, while others may try to make me feel better by downplaying what happened to me, or even sticking up for the person who wronged me. But that's beside the point. Should I burden my sweet-tempered friends with my complaints? Surely they have problems of their own and could use uplifting messages instead of toxin from the likes of me!

I've (mostly) broken myself of the habit of passive aggressively venting my every petty complaint, and even my deeper (angrier) rants, onto innocent bystanders. I break the rules less and less often because I cringe when I do it. The longer I practice positive social habits, the easier it becomes to keep up the good work because I'm aware that what I'm doing is wrong.

As for venting about my spouse and children, I have never made a practice of this. I don't say anything behind my family's backs that I can't say to their faces. I consider this line that I don't cross as one of the reasons why I've been married for over twenty-five years and why I have a close relationship with all three of my children. If you haven't created this boundary, do so today! It's never too late to break bad habits.

But why isn't it fair game when we rant about people we don't even know, or about institutions like the government? What's the harm when everyone else is doing it? Comedians have built careers on mockery, satire and sarcasm! Well, that's exactly the reason why I avoid being snarky. Everyone else is doing it. Do we need more anger?

I love comedy, but I'm weary of toxic material. I've realized that I end up feeling keyed up, even while laughing. I want an escape from the madness, not an incitement to riot! When comedy doesn't leave me feeling good, but instead inspires me to add my own angry jokes to the mix, it's not funny anymore. It's easier to tear down than it is to build up— most of us can be comedians without much effort. Talented comics are capable of being funny without being mean.. Think of famous comics throughout the years. It's not the easy hateful comedy that lasts, but the original acts that become classics. Unfortunately, we live in a world where being hateful is easy entertainment and we've lost many of our greatest comedic talents. It's up to us to realize that we don't enjoy hate anymore. Stop supporting it.

I'm smiling as I remember my favorite classic comedy bits, and not one of them is hateful. Who doesn't laugh every Christmas when the squirrel terrorizes the Griswald family? We could all use "more cow bell" (*Saturday Night Live*). Or how about doing "the mess around"? I've watched *Plains, Trains and Automobiles* dozens of times. The scene when

John Candy drives while Steve Martin sleeps wins every time.

Yes, of course comedians are capable of making us laugh without resorting to bottom-feeder humor, and so can we! I've made it a personal challenge to be socially fun without being toxic. I slip into my old bad habits sometimes. A change in attitude and behavior is a process. The point I'm making in this section is that sometimes we contribute to a hateful world because it's fun. That's sad to realize, isn't it? Why are we hated? One reason why we are hated is because we are haters ourselves! The less we hate, the less we'll be hated---sort of. We can't control everything that happens to us. It's often no fault of our own when we are hated.

Why do we have an epidemic of bullying? Haven't we always had a bullying problem? Is the problem worse now, or are we simply noticing it more? After all, when bullying leads to suicide and mass violence, it does tend to get people's attention. We also see bullying playing out in public through video cameras and the Internet. Maybe we are simply more aware of it, and the public nature of this has escalated the problem.

Hate has always been with us, always. Think of slavery, think of cross burning, think of the Holocaust, think of all the dark and twisted serial killers and rapists throughout history, think of monsters, dictators, and abusers. Evil has been alive and well always. There is nothing new under the sun.

But time passes on, and with it, new technology is created. Now the whole planet is plugged in. We can fly anywhere in the world, from cities that never sleep, to jungle villages and remote islands. We can communicate at any time, with anyone in the world. We have phones in more places than ever before. We have television, radio, and all manner of communication. Our ability to connect is amazing... and horrifying!

We can sit around and sing about how we are all the same, except that we are not. Some of us are better than others. Some of us are worse than others. I believe that it is helpful to admit that evil exists. Let's take the mystery out of it and not give it any more power than it deserves. Evil craves power—why should we make it easier to take it from us?

Evil has created problems throughout history. Monsters often have a perverted reality, either due to madness or to an appetite for depravity, or perhaps those two ideas mean the same thing. Regardless of what motivates a deranged person, we can identify them as dangerous. But why do seemingly normal people do evil things?

Why do citizens obey immoral commands issued by a corrupt government? Why do bystanders passively step aside when bullies attack? Why do our friends choose to "stay out of it" when someone hurts us? Am I hitting closer to home now?

You probably don't feel hated by a monster. And you probably don't suffer from a serious case of bullying either, although you might know of someone who is. If I had to guess, you feel hated by the people you meet in your everyday life.

You might have more insight into why this is happening to you than you realize. Think about your personal history with your haters. When you feel hurt by someone, what is the context?

I've mentioned controversial topics before, but it bears repeating. If you discuss politics, religion, education, parenting, health care, alternative medicine, activism, social problems, literature, music, television, movies, or virtually any topic that anyone, anywhere, at any point in time and space, may have an opinion about, you will draw haters. This shouldn't surprise us.

Nonetheless, this is not acceptable! Perpetual dissention, bickering, carping, rhetoric, and an overall unsupportive toxic response to anything we say is unacceptable. Don't let anyone tell you that this is just how people are, and that it's somehow your fault for asserting an opinion.

Here are two examples: Did you expect a debate when you told a friend that you were having a high-risk surgery? Did you want a debate when you told your neighbor that you can't afford newly imposed taxes? No. You expected sympathy.

So when your friend launched on a long tirade about how you should avoid surgery by exploring natural remedies, you were taken aback (or flip this around the other way: you explained to your friend that you are trying natural remedies to avoid surgery and your friend criticized your decision). In the taxes example, you wanted sympathy about your financial hardship, and instead you got an earful about politics—to the point of blaming you for your position, even though your complaint is based on real harm and not ideology. No, when you share your concerns about your health or finances, you don't expect a debate (unless you've become cynical, like I admit to being).

When we share our lives with people, we don't always anticipate a debate about issues. We expect a supportive response to us personally. If I post about my homeschooled child, for example, someone may assert that homeschooled children are social misfits. Arguing the issue of homeschooling, when I'm talking about my child, is inappropriate. Don't tell me that my baby is a misfit! Why would you do that? What business is it of yours anyway? Did I say that I had a problem? And don't you trust me to know how to take care of my family? A debate about the issue of homeschooling feels like an attack on me personally, especially if the debate occurs when I've shared something about my own family.

Apply that same scenario to the two examples I gave earlier. If we share that we have an upcoming surgery, we are expecting sympathy, support, and maybe even an offer of help. We probably aren't expecting a debate on the necessity of the surgery in question, of conventional medicine, or on the politics of health insurance.

And don't get me started on taxes. We can't complain about financial hardship without inviting judgment about our situation. Perhaps we should get a "real job" and not stay home with the kids. Perhaps we should get a "better" job. Perhaps we should go back to school. Oh, it's the government's fault. It's the left's fault. It's the right's fault.

Haters don't want to hear our problems. They don't want to be bothered to help someone else. They don't want to feel awkward. They don't want to do any extra work. They don't want to even be bothered to care.

You might be flinching right about now. You might be thinking, "I don't feel comfortable calling my friends 'haters'." If that's what you are feeling, I challenge you to look at the situation objectively. The opposite of love is hate. It's not love that bickers, tears down, resents, ignores, inflames, and rejects.

It may be easier to talk about haters in an abstract sort of way, but the truth is, hate affects us the most when it's close to home. We aren't all that hurt, at least not for long, when strangers say something stupid or mean. We also aren't personally affronted when the government, a celebrity, or some other public figure says something negative or hostile. We don't take these things personally. No, it's when our *family and friends* do it that we bleed.

I'm not saying that people shouldn't discuss issues, but why air these things out in a way that attacks our family and friends? We perpetuate a never-ending, ever-escalating cycle of negativity every time we rant, vent, or debate an issue. How many opinions do we need in this world, haven't we heard enough on every possible subject by now? In my opinion (yes, I recognize the irony), we have more than enough critics.

Have you guessed where I'm headed with this? Our haters are… us. We are the haters. Let's face it, the problem is rampant. It's happening so often that we're *all* guilty of being a hater at one time or another.

On the small end of the scale, think about a time when your friend posted about a problem and you pretended not to see it. Maybe your friend's timing was inconvenient. Maybe your friend is annoying. Maybe your friend has other friends who can help, so why should you be bothered? Most of us have friends who ask for help too often, right? Whatever the reason, I think all of us are guilty of doing nothing at all when someone needs us. Hopefully we don't slip away from our responsibilities to our family, friends, neighbors, and community too often, hopefully not. But are we always on top of things? No, I can't imagine that we are. I know that I'm not. Sometimes I'm a poor excuse for a friend.

The truth is, if we want to understand our haters, we have to look at ourselves. Are we ever angry? Are we ever impatient? Do we ever walk away when we know that we should help someone? If we look into why we are angry, unsupportive, disrespectful and downright hateful, we'll gain insight into how we can improve our response to negativity.

Remember, by the end of this book we'll be talking not only about surviving in a hateful world, but *thriving*. If we hope to thrive in a hateful world, we need to break ourselves out of the rut we are in. Generalities and musings about love and hate are not as helpful as specific definitions and instructions. A good way to work on abstract concepts is to use philosophy and logic.

1 Corinthians 13:4-8

New International Version (NIV)

4 **Love is patient, love is kind. It does not envy, it does not boast, it is not proud. 5 It does not dishonor others, it is not self-seeking, it is not easily angered, it keeps no record of wrongs. 6 Love does not delight in evil but rejoices with the truth. 7 It always protects, always trusts, always hopes, always perseveres.**

It's logical then, that if we reverse this definition of love, we now have a definition of hate that is clear and concise.

Hate is impatient.

Hate is unkind.

Hate envies.

Hate boasts.

Hate is proud.

Hate dishonors others.

Hate is self-seeking.

Hate is easily angered.

Hate keeps a record of wrongs.

Hate delights in evil.

Hate rejoices with lies.

Hate never protects.

Hate never trusts.

Hate never hopes.

Hate never perseveres.

And there we have it. This is a list of things that haters do. Does this list, laid out simply and clearly in black and white terms clarify your situation for you? You are surrounded by haters, and sometimes you yourself are tempted to be one.

You are not a hater unless you act on your negative feelings, but all of us can understand the heart of a hater, to some extent, from our own experiences as human beings. There's not one of us who hasn't at one time or another felt impatient. Agree? That's an easy one to fess up to. If we wait at the grocery counter long enough we'll eventually become impatient with whoever is holding up the line. The line doesn't even need to be that long—some of us have a short fuse and are impatient on a regular basis.

We can run down the entire list of hateful actions, but I think you get my point. We can sympathize with negative emotions, since we are all human, and we've experienced many of these unpleasant dark feelings ourselves. To feel is to be human, and we can't control that. To act on our feelings is a different story. Our choices (assuming that we are of healthy mind) are not controlled by emotional response alone, but by free will.

Now imagine that our haters have no moral compass. That little voice that tells you to keep your mouth shut? That nagging feeling in your heart that says, "oh don't do that, it would be unkind"? Our haters don't have a moral compass or a kind heart—they don't want it, they don't seek it, they don't *have* it.

Should we get into why our haters lack these things? No, we should not. It doesn't matter for the purpose of this book. Why people do what they do on a fundamental level is not a riddle we should waste time on. Let the psychologists try to puzzle this one out. The only "why" that we need to focus on is the "why do they hate **me**" part. Why they hate in general is a big philosophical and possibly medical question. Why they hate us in particular is the part we need to know something about.

What do we do that triggers haters? I'm not saying that we are at fault, only that we might be putting ourselves needlessly in the line of fire. Haters will continue hurting people

105

until the end of time. So what can we do about it? Why should we care about what haters say?

Love perseveres and hate does not. We shouldn't care what haters say, but sometimes we fail in our efforts to shrug off negativity. The world is hateful. But we can thrive anyway. Love always trusts and always hopes.

5

GOOD IS BAD

HATERS CONFUSE

Haters don't rejoice in the truth, remember? They lie. They lie in their actions, they lie in their words. So why do we let them influence us? Why do we listen to what they say? Why do we get so confused? Haters confuse us from our life's purpose and everything we know in our hearts to be true, because we are human. When haters hurt us, we are thrown off course. Suddenly we wonder if the haters are right. Maybe we aren't good enough. Maybe we don't know what we're doing after all. Maybe our ideas won't work. Maybe they are right and we are wrong.

Haters enjoy confusion, remember? They don't rejoice in the truth. When you are weak you are no longer a threat to them. They can walk all over you and feel better about themselves. Haters enjoy power. They enjoy control. They are unkind. Remember all of these things because it's terribly hard to stay focused when haters tear us down.

Haters have a way of saying that good things are bad, and bad things are good. They say it loudly, often, and with such authority. They are arrogant. They repeat the same lies over and over again until we are worn down. We begin to question if maybe we aren't seeing things clearly. Maybe they are right. Maybe what we thought is good is bad. Maybe what we thought was bad was good.

Whoa! Shake off the hypnosis! Step back if you begin to second guess yourself. Haven't you ever heard that the first answer you come up with on an exam is probably the correct one? If you don't feel sure about an answer, go with your first guess. I think we can apply that here as well. If your gut is telling you that something is good, don't let haters change your answer.

Obviously we are wrong sometimes. If I'm truly confused, and I want to make sure that I'm keeping an open mind, I step away from the haters and I do my own research on the issue. I find a balance of information and then I make up my own mind. I keep my own council! I don't let naysayers persuade me.

Listening to haters is a slippery slope. We have to know when we are keeping an open mind and when we are allowing ourselves to be misled. Sometimes it's hard to know the difference. What works for me is prayer, reading objective information, and then stepping back from the issue until a later date.

When I re-examine the issue with a fresh perspective my focus is much clearer.

You might remember the article I shared in Chapter Two about my journey as an artist? My college art professor had given me a hard time without just cause. Years later, hindsight is twenty-twenty, or at least closer to perfect vision. If this had happened to me today, I wouldn't have made a life changing decision based on what haters say.

My professor had a taste for dark art and "chaos" to the point of scoffing at any other tradition. He ridiculed me by telling me that I probably like symmetry. He looked me straight in the eyes and said "You are not an artist." My professor was also rumored to be having an affair with one of my fellow students.

His credibility with me should have been absolutely zero! Why didn't I trust myself? I don't share his taste in art, I don't respect teachers who have affairs with their students, especially given the age difference between the two of them, and I happen to like symmetry.

Why then couldn't I see that I shouldn't listen to this hater?

As you might recall from the article, I'm sorry to say that I quit my art major at the end of that semester. I couldn't escape my humiliation and misery fast enough. It didn't matter how many other people in my life had told me how talented I was. No, all I heard were my haters' voices.

I'd had a wonderfully supportive high school art teacher. My confidence soared in her classes. Why didn't I think about her, and the time that she had invested in me? I also had family and friends who had encouraged me. But here I was, a young college student, quitting art all because of my haters, my professor and his eager-to-please student critics.

My fellow students had caught on early in the semester to what style of art the professor preferred, and which students delivered what he liked. Those students received glowing praise not only from the professor, but from the student critics. My peers also knew the style he didn't care for, and which students the professor had taken a personal dislike to. I was one of those students. Every critique session was torture because I knew that the professor would demean my work and my personality, and my peers would jump on the bandwagon in an attempt to sound superior.

I followed all assignments to the letter and I worked hard. I was an anxious student, which seemed to annoy my professor all the more. His harassment of me was purely subjective, as there was nothing specific that I did wrong. There was no justification for the hostility toward me.

Meanwhile, many of my peers' work could be summed up like this: "I did it at the last minute after a night of partying, I didn't follow the assignment, I'm marketing this project as 'chaos born of darkness' to cover for the fact that I threw this together, and I know I'll not only get away with it, but I'll get an A". But even though I could see for myself that my fellow students were churning out inferior work I doubted myself. I began to see that bad was good, and that good was bad. They were good. I was bad. After all, how could I be right when the entire class believed the same as the professor did?

Well, I'm all grown up now and it's not difficult to sort this out. The professor was a cynical person who was edgy and popular. There was something dark and mysterious about him that appealed to college students. I was unfortunately one of his victims, but it was nothing personal. I doubt this man remembers me. What a shame that I gave his words such importance when it probably meant nothing at all to him.

This story has a happy ending, as was already mentioned in the article. I've moved on from my early experiences and my oil paintings have been featured in galleries and exhibits. That's not why I brought this up though. I'm referring to this incident because it's a good example of how **haters confuse us**.

I was confused and distracted from my life's purpose. Just think of all the lost opportunities! I didn't take up art again until later in life, much later. It's a shame. How many other artists have stopped creating art because of haters?

And why stop at artists? Apply this example to every dreamer, activist, and student; to all of us who want to make a difference and bring something new to this world! We all have a purpose in life and haters confuse us about what that purpose is. If we believe that we aren't good enough, we might give up. We might lose our way.

Don't let haters confuse you when you make decisions. Do your own research and seek valid information, but don't listen to haters! If your heart is telling you—if *God* is telling you—that you are on the right course, don't let haters confuse you!

Haters like to tear people down instead of building people up. If those who argue against you are tearing you down, that's a red flag that your critic is not helping you improve, as much as he/she is tearing you down unproductively.

But what if your naysayer is giving you constructive criticism? Seek impartial resources. Explore your options. Sometimes we assume that people who criticize us are being hateful, when they are actually giving us valuable feedback. Book reviewers have pointed out mistakes in my writing and I've used their comments to improve my craft. A professional takes criticism on the chin, and the same is true for accepting advice for personal self-improvement.

Use discernment to determine if your critic is offering you anything of value. Ask "Is this person providing me with specifics about what I need to improve, and/or suggestions on how to improve?" If all you are hearing is that you are bad, without any explanation, and without any tips for how to improve, chances are that your critic is a hater and not a legitimate critic.

Another thing to keep in mind is that your haters don't get to decide when you should throw in the towel, only you can do that. Maybe you've taken on something that isn't working out for you. If that's your situation, you can decide to dig deeper and try harder, or you can let go of it and move on to something else. There's no shame in changing your mind, but don't let haters do it for you.

Haters don't necessarily interact with us personally. Sometimes the negative messages reach us through television personalities, talk radio, or the Internet. Are they giving you an opinion or verifiable information? Are you feeling stressed and negative about the future after listening to these personalities? Fact-check everything you hear. Haters are self-serving and they don't rejoice in the truth. Learn how to recognize propaganda, spin and even satire. What passes for "news" is often biased or outright false. Recognize when you're being played.

Hate and drama sells. I remind myself of this when I get caught up in news events, especially if oppression, corruption or injustice is involved. I coach myself to calm down and sort the facts from the fiction. If the haters that get you the most stirred up are on television, turn off the TV. Take a break from it. If your haters are on the Internet, unplug. I give myself breaks from the noise. Educate yourself. Follow your own heart and listen to what you know to be true. Don't let the haters confuse you!

NATALIE BUSKE THOMAS

6

CLEAR AND PRESENT DANGER

So far we've been talking about haters that are hurtful to the spirit but harmless to the body. I'd be irresponsible if my sole advice to you was to say "don't let the haters confuse you", and basically "ignore the haters". Haters are bullies and sometimes standing up to a bully is a good strategy. Other times standing up to a bully will get you killed. Haters can be stalkers and abusers and worse. Please know that even if your haters seem harmless, they may in fact be dangerous. Ignoring a clear and present danger can be deadly.

Haters threaten our emotional security, our financial security, and our physical security. I don't want to scare you, but I do want to urge you to use precautionary measures when dealing with haters. Assume that anyone, at any time, in any situation, can be dangerous. Sometimes threats are not empty. I'd be irresponsible if I didn't include a chapter on personal safety.

Think about how much energy it takes to sustain malice. It must be exhausting to be angry and hostile all the time! And yet some haters overachieve. They have seemingly boundless energy to make people miserable. Do your best to avoid and diffuse unwanted attention.

Don't make eye contact with a stranger who seems "off". Trust your intuition.

Don't answer hate mail. Don't respond to hateful remarks on social media.

Don't announce where you are, don't post photos that reveal where you live, and don't broadcast when you won't be home.

When you feel afraid of someone, there's probably a good reason for that feeling. Don't draw attention to yourself by interacting with your hater.

Minimize Your Chances of Being Stalked Online

1) Don't make a habit of posting on public forums.

2) If you notice that someone is focusing on you, take a break from social media for a while (or at least from that forum). Chances are, your hater will become bored and will move on.

3) Seek ways to avoid your hater that won't inform him/her of what you have done. Often haters will respond poorly if you "block" them. They might even rally their friends together to actively bully you online. If you can't unfollow your hater quietly, consider dropping your account or at least lying low for a while. You may find that simply by changing your schedule you'll avoid interacting with your hater.

4) If online threats are of a serious nature you can report your hater to the FBI Cybercrime division (or the equivalent if you live outside of the United States). You can threaten legal action as well. These are things that I have done on behalf of one of my children. It solved the problem immediately and it was, I must confess, quite satisfying as well. I won't provide any more detail than this, because I am not a lawyer and I'm not qualified to give you legal advice. All I'm saying is that you can seek official and legal ways to respond if your hater (or your child's hater) doesn't leave you alone.

I've focused on Internet bullying, but I know that some of you deal with haters up close and personal in your everyday lives. I too have people in my life who are toxic and harmful. I've even tried, unsuccessfully, to hide from these people by moving without telling them my new address or phone number. They found me.

What do we do when haters literally turn up on our doorstep? Well, keep a cool head. This is one time when deception is A-OK and probably necessary. Say what you need to say to get your haters out of your home as soon as you can without the situation escalating. Get a message out to someone you trust that you need help.

Tell people about the haters in your life. Do you fear anyone? Let people know! Take martial arts, a personal safety class, or a self-defense course. Educate yourself on how to recognize personal safety risks.

If you're in danger: Alert the police. Get a restraining order. Move away. Move farther away. Hide. I don't know your situation. But I won't tell you that no one can really hurt you. Of course they can! Listen to your intuition.

Assume that people can be dangerous. It's a scary world out there and I sure don't want any of us to get hurt. This book is not about standing up to bullies or about taking the law into your own hands.

This book is about empowering you to thrive, despite the obstacles that negative people put in our paths. We need to maintain a healthy respect for evil and keep our distance. Haters threaten. We need to take that message seriously even if nothing ever comes of it. Don't poke a stick at a bear!

NATALIE BUSKE THOMAS

7

TURN OFF THEIR MIC

I don't have a PhD in anything. But I've thrived in a hateful world, and I believe that I can help you. So much of thriving is about attitude, as everyone says. What most people don't explain is how we can have a positive attitude when life feels anything but positive. I'll share with you one of the low points in my life and its impact on me.

When I was fifteen years old I was in a whitewater rafting accident. A doctor said that

I'd be in a wheelchair for the rest of my life. I danced in my next recital.

That's the short version of the story. Now I'll share a longer version, beginning with my own words as I wrote them when I was sixteen. When I was cleaning out my mother's apartment I stumbled upon the issue of my high school magazine that had published my rafting accident story.

As published in *Voice* magazine, May 1986.

My Whitewater Rafting Accident

"The grass tickled my bare legs as Esther and I dragged the rubber raft down the slope to the river. We were disappointed by the cold air and overcast sky, but were excited to meet the challenge of the rapids.

The first part of the trip we raced against the others of our group. Soon everyone was wet from the splashing and tipping of rafts. Whenever we started to dry off, someone was sure to get us wet again.

The second section of the trip we hit the rapids. We were serious as we maneuvered our raft around the rocks. It was raining lightly and the water was wild. It slapped the rocks and pushed the raft wherever it wanted.

The raft next to ours struck a boulder and flipped over. James was unable to get back into it and was caught in the current. I was steering the raft and was close enough to pull James into our raft. The extra weight caused it to hit bottom occasionally. I was worried that the jagged rocks would rip the lining. The undying power of the river knocked us into the rocks time and time again. I used my legs to shove off when we were wedged in between boulders. We were feeling pretty cocky at how adept we were at rafting. After all, it was my third year and Esther's fourth.

The raft was free now and was headed directly for a tree that hung over the river bank. The orange raft squeezed itself under the limb. We jumped for the tree in what seemed like slow motion. My legs were being sucked under, but I clung to the branch. Esther was at the tip of the limb and partially in the water. She was able to meet the raft as it hurled down the rapids. James was also low on the limb and was able to join a different raft. Since I had been steering, I ended up high on the limb. Wrapped around the branch, I looked below at the jagged rocks and swirling water. I didn't see any rafts coming and it didn't look too wise to jump down. I snaked across the limb to the other side. Although the woods were dense, I knew if I kept a straight path I would eventually reach a road.

I was right, but it was after two hours and bloody legs. The mosquitos feasted on my bare skin and the gnats swarmed around the many cuts I was getting from the thorns and brambles. At first I was careful about where I stepped, but as I grew more frightened, I ran almost blindly. It was now pouring, which made it difficult to see. When I finally made it to the road, I was picked up by a fellow camper. I got a ride to the rafting bus.

. . .

I went to a specialist in Fort Wayne who immediately put me on seizure medication. I was on the medication for two weeks. My seizures increased both in frequency and duration. They became more painful and I was weak for a long time afterward. I started a new problem with slurred or stuttering speech. I was so weak and drugged, I could not walk the length of a room without aid.

...

I acted like I was asleep with my eyes open. The specialist, a neurologist, put me on new medication. I felt less out of it, but it did nothing to control the seizures. In fact, I had the worst spell ever. It lasted for two hours; it was very painful and I had trouble breathing.

When this medication didn't work, the specialist gave me another EEG test which I consider an experience guaranteed to make anyone feel like a freak. This time the test was negative. I took a cat scan which was terrifying. My head was strapped to a table while I was put in a huge x-ray tube. The test came back negative. Now the doctor was completely baffled and stuck me in the hospital. I guess that's what they do when they don't know what else to do with you.

...

At that time I was having about three seizures daily. I was very angry. I was back to where I started from. I had missed over six weeks of school, the school Valentine's dance, being in the play, going to my dance classes, and youth group for what seemed like no reason."

~

Yes, doctors had missed the mark on this one. I had been repeatedly asked if I had hit my head on the tree. I assured them that I had not. "It's possible that you don't remember hitting your head," one of them said. No, I would have remembered hitting my head, I insisted. They didn't listen.

I was admitted, tested like a lab rat, and released from the hospital. I was in and out of doctor's offices. My seizures continued and escalated until I was too weak to walk. I was brought into a doctor's appointment via a borrowed wheelchair when I overhead a doctor proclaim that one day I wasn't going to leave that chair. I'd be in it for the rest of my life.

Fortunately my young self never believed this. I refused to accept that my seizures would render me an invalid. I was a dancer! I didn't know how it would all work out, but I didn't doubt that it would. I resumed as many of my activities as I could, beginning with attending church.

I had a seizure during the service. I was mortified! The good news is that I never lost consciousness during these seizures, which is why doctors were mixed on calling these shaking spells seizures at all. The spells caused violent spasms of mainly my legs. During severe spells my arms were somewhat affected. After the spells ended, my muscles were weak, even the muscles in my hands. I could barely grip a pencil after a long spell.

I knew when a seizure was about to happen because I felt an uncomfortable sensation in my back, as if my body was being squeezed. I usually had time to get myself to a private space before the worst of the shaking started. This is what I did during the church service.

My boyfriend (who later became my husband) helped me into the foyer in the nick of time. The shaking was severe enough that I ended up on the floor, as spastic as a fish out of water. A member of the congregation appeared and asked if he could help. He said he was a chiropractor. I agreed to let him try, but I had no respect for chiropractic care.

Lo and behold, all he did is pinch the nerves between my neck and my shoulder and the seizure stopped dead! I couldn't believe it. No one had been able to stop my seizures before. Spiritual person that I am, of course I found it significant that this miracle had occurred in a church, of all places! I began chiropractic treatments right away.

That solved the problem—permanently! I still need to pop in for a treatment now and then, especially if I've agitated my neck. My chiropractor actually listened to me. He wanted to know every detail of what happened during my rafting accident, and unlike the doctors who refused to listen, he believed me when I said that I didn't hit my head.

He especially paid attention when he heard me describe that my legs were being sucked under the tree limb by the current. I was relaying how I was scared that I would fall in the river, onto the rocks below. He asked more questions and he nodded when I said that it was hard to pull myself completely out of the river because my lower body was being swept under the branch by the current. I won the battle though and I successfully made it out of the river, onto the branch, and then I climbed the tree to dry land.

My chiropractor zeroed in on the part when my lower body was pulled with great force at an unnatural angle. He explained spinal injury and other issues that I admit are fuzzy to me now. All I know is that the treatments worked!

Now that I've told you the story of my whitewater rafting accident, I can bring us around to the point of this chapter: Turn off your haters' microphones. When a noisy person doesn't have a mic, we can still hear their voice but at least it's not amplified above everyone else. I can't stop haters from talking, but I can turn off their mic. Why let their voices ring louder in my ears than the voices of people who support me?

When I wrote the story of my accident I could choose what was important to tell. I'm proud of my sixteen year old self because I left out parts of the story, including some of the people who were a part of what happened. I didn't mention one of my haters at all. I made a conscious decision that this person was not important enough to make it into my story. And that's what I want to impress upon you. You are the writer of your own story and you get to decide who makes the cut, and who doesn't.

The person I had left out of my story was a camp counselor who made the comment that if I were her daughter I'd be spanked for leaving the area and making people worry, searching for me in the river. I was stunned when I heard this. It never occurred to me that anyone would think that I had done something wrong. I was embarrassed and humiliated. I had expected that my counselors would have been impressed with my bravery. I had been through a terrifying ordeal. At the very least, when they saw me bedraggled, bloodied, soaked, and convulsing in spasms that would later develop into an expensive and harrowing medical ordeal, anger should have turned into compassion.

My hater didn't know what had happened to me, only that I hadn't been in the river at all. She was thinking of the safety of the search party, and understandably she was outraged that people were putting their own lives at risk needlessly. But if she had stopped to think about her words before saying them, maybe she wouldn't have said something that I still remember, almost thirty years later.

I was judged unfairly. I'm glad that my younger self understood that this hater's microphone needed to be turned off. Nonetheless, she was noisy enough to be heard. I'm not saying that haters won't hurt us, they will. I remember the sting of her words vividly decades later. I was relieved to be back at the camp, alive. I was hurting. The last thing I needed was to be condemned!

Because the camp had never called my parents after the accident, they had no idea what had happened to me. They were shocked by my appearance when I came home. There wasn't a square inch of skin on my legs that wasn't marred by cuts. I was white as a sheet. I was skinny as a rail.

I was resilient. Even after my father died and my seizures were a medical crisis, I viewed these hardships as temporary. I knew that I'd heal from grief. I knew that I'd bounce back from my rafting accident. I was right.

Years later, the accident was a distant memory. I had gotten married and was living in Germany where Brent was stationed with the U.S. Army. My mom phoned to say that someone named James had called asking for me. She told him that I was married now and living overseas. At first I couldn't recall who James was. Oh yes, he was the boy at camp that day in the river, the one I pulled into my raft.

As an adult I see the story of my accident through the eyes of a mother. Not only had I managed to make it out of a dangerous situation alive, but I found my way back to the camp bus. I had saved James from serious injury or even death. I was a hero! If this had been my daughter I would have been so relieved to see that she was safe. I would have hugged her. Shame on the camp counselor for saying that if I were her daughter I would have been spanked!

There are five points I want to make about what I just said:

1) I am kinder to myself when I imagine if the same thing had happened to one of my daughters. I'd never condemn my daughters! **Why then should I condemn myself, or allow anyone else to do so?**

2) When James had fallen out of his raft I risked my own safety on that river without a second thought. Of course I was young then, and reckless. But if the same thing had happened today, I would do it all over again because *it was the right thing to do*. **When helping others is part of our make-up, we live without regrets.**

3) May this encourage you! Many people will do the right thing and might not even remember it later. We'll never hear most of these stories. **The world is a hateful place,**

but there are good people to help us through it. Earthly, and I believe heavenly, angels are all around us. We don't always know that they are there.

4) The negativity surrounding my whitewater rafting accident is remembered (i.e. the doctors who didn't listen to me and the camp counselor who judged me), but I'm not haunted by my past. I got married and moved on to exciting new adventures less than three years after my rafting accident. **Haters can't hold us back from the happy life we are meant to live!**

5) My adult experiences with haters are much more complicated than illustrated by this whitewater rafting accident, but the same principles apply. Imagine a cold, wet, exhausted, bleeding child—lost, alone, and afraid. Isn't that how we feel when we are under attack? **Give yourself mercy and grace even when no one else will.**

142

Most of us muddle through life doing the best that we can. We are misunderstood. We make mistakes. Instead of receiving mercy and grace, we're often knocked down by haters. We're criticized and judged when we need love and support the most.

We get distracted by those who don't support us, instead of focusing on those who do. Strain your ears to hear the whispers of those worth hearing. Sometimes there are not two sides to a story, there is only one—the *right* one! When one side is acting hatefully and the other side is doing nothing wrong, there is only one side.

The world tells us that we should listen to all sides of an argument and support a balanced report. I'm all for this concept of fairness and objectivity if two sides really do exist. In my experience, this isn't always the truth. Sometimes the Emperor has no clothes! There is a right and a wrong, a good and a bad. When we give haters "balance", what we're really doing is tipping the scales to help them win. *Haters do not deserve a voice.* Turn off their microphones!

At one time or another, all of us are capable of hurting each other. Our response to a messy and hateful world is critical. If we put more toxin in, we'll get more toxin out. We already know that the world is full of problems and we don't need more people condemning everything that is wrong with the world. What we need is a loving response. Hate perpetuates hate. Love solves problems.

Love is patient.

Love is kind.

Love does not envy.

Love does not boast.

Love is not proud.

Love does not dishonor others.

Love is not self-seeking.

Love is not easily angered.

Love keeps no record of wrongs.

Love does not delight in evil.

Love rejoices with the truth.

Love always protects.

Love always trusts.

Love always hopes.

Love always perseveres.

If we consider toxic debate a form of entertainment, we're not responding to hate with love. We're adding more hate to hate.

Turn off Their Microphone

1) Don't participate in toxic conversations. Walk away as quickly as you can if you've become part of one by accident.

Love keeps no record of wrongs. As tempting as it is for me to press forward until I win an argument, it's clear that love doesn't keep a record of wrongs. If I'm not keeping score, it's not important to win. When there is a choice between being right and being kind, love dictates that I must be kind.

I have a hard time letting go of a conversation that makes me feel as if I've been misunderstood and misjudged. I want to set the record straight. I want to explain what I meant. I want others to believe and support my side of the argument. I want to dispel anything that isn't true about me. I especially hate it when I know that I'm right, but I have to let the matter drop because the conversation has taken an ugly turn.

2) Let go of arguments. Resist the temptation to defend yourself or your position. Make a graceful exit.

Have faith that the truth will be come to light on its own. You probably can't change anyone's mind anyway. Trust that wrongs will be righted—the truth has a way of coming out. Walk away.

3) When walking away is not an option, respond with patience instead of anger.

Never allow yourself the excuse that you're an impatient person or a hothead. We all are! Sure, it might be more difficult for people with poor impulse control to stay on track, but trust me, none of us are perfect. We are impatient and hotheaded by nature; even us mellow types can get plenty riled up.

It's our responsibility to control ourselves the best that we can, and to work hard at being patient. Have more patience, don't snap off so easily. Less anger means less stress, which means better health. Act better, feel better.

Love is not easily angered. Love is patient. An awareness of these two simple rules for love helps me stay on course. If I let my temper flare at the slightest trigger, I'm not acting in love. If I'm impatient with my neighbor, I'm not acting in love. I try, but I'm far from perfect.

When my son was little I tried to get him to do his math homework. I left him with his math book and a blank notebook for a good hour. He was quiet and he didn't move from his chair, so I had assumed that he must be working hard. He was not. He had done literally nothing! He was exactly as I had left him – his book was open to the same page and his notebook was still blank. He hadn't done anything!

I tried to get to the bottom of it. Had he been defying me or did he have a learning disability? What was going on? My conversation with him was frustrating to say the least. It escalated into a meltdown and a pencil was thrown in a fit of anger. The pencil landed at the exact angle to embed itself into the wall. My son still giggles over this incident, because the meltdown was mine.

I apologized. I was not acting in a loving way. I was not patient. I was quick to anger.

4) The more loving you become, the easier it will be to heal from hateful situations.

If you want to thrive in a hateful world, you have to do much more than deflect or prevent haters from getting under your skin. You have to do more than respond to haters. You have to do more than walk away from haters. You have to work on *yourself.* You have to become a person of love.

NATALIE BUSKE THOMAS

8

DEFINE SUCCESS

"I have arrived! Let the show begin!" This was the line that my youngest daughter Savannah said on stage during a musical when she was about eight years old. It was one of the show's highlights because she delivered the line loudly, clearly, and with a joyful flourish. The audience roared. Her red sparkly costume and naturally curly hair added to her star power. This is the confidence that we should all strive for.

151

The show is just getting started. It's time to make our dreams come true. It's time to savor all of the successes we've already achieved. It's time for gratitude. It's time for healing. It's time to be happy. No matter what the world throws at us, we are unsinkable.

Happiness is in the beauty of the stars, the unconditional love of animals, the innocence of babies, and the fragility of flowers. We're in agreement about many things, we humans on planet Earth. We respond in a similar way to colors, odors and sounds. We even like a lot of the same foods. We enjoy the sound of the ocean, the colors of a rainbow, and the sight of an eagle in flight. We want to love and be loved. We dream. We long to be free.

This writing assignment by my son Nicholas expresses this well. He was fourteen years old when he wrote "Flight".

FLIGHT

"I'm soaring through the air, like I've always done before; nothing unusual, but different every time. The wind is in my face and my feathers flap back and forth from the velocity of my glorious flight. I look down and see the treetops of the forest, and some other birds I know. Soon the scenery changes and I am over the rapids, full of salmon. They lead to a smaller, calmer river where I stop for a drink. After I guzzle down a few beak-fulls, I decide to go farther. I flap my wings rapidly and soon I am back in the warm summer air."

~

I've often dreamt about flying, but my dream-flying is usually horrible. I struggle to stay airborne, which is the story of my life. I'm going to share that story with you now, the condensed version anyway.

I was born in upstate New York and brought home to a two bedroom house where about a dozen people lived under the same roof. I was born a "blue baby" requiring oxygen. As a newborn and an infant I had whooping cough multiple times. Mom thought I was going to die.

My dad was in the Vietnam War, so Mom had moved back home. That's how I came to live at Grandma and Grandpa's house for most of the first year of my life. Grandpa worked at Nestlé chocolate factory. Grandma stayed home and raised their nine children.

When my father returned from the war we moved into a mobile home near Grissom Air Force Base, located about twelve miles from Kokomo, Indiana. When I was a toddler I suffered a head injury that cracked my skull. Mom and Dad worried that I might not make it. Obviously I survived. I have no sense of direction whatsoever. I'm hopelessly lost if I go around the corner of a familiar street in my own neighborhood. I assume those things are related, but maybe not.

Dad stayed in the Air Force for several more years, and then was deployed for a second tour in the Vietnam War. We'll never know for sure if that's how he ended up with terminal cancer, but that's my assumption.

Dad was first diagnosed with cancer when he was about twenty-nine or so. He beat cancer that first time around. Then it came back, five years after his cancer treatments and final all-clear. This time, Dad would not be so fortunate.

It's hard to remember what it felt like to be a teenage girl not only losing her father, but watching him die a slow and painful death. I know that somewhere deep inside me those memories are buried. They are part of who I am.

I found an old essay I wrote for my high school creative writing class in the stack of old papers that Mom had kept. I could only find one page of the essay. I suppose I'm grateful that I don't have the rest of this, as it's uncomfortable to read.

At Church with Dad

"I lean against the side of the pew so I can see the pastor. He's telling the congregation to pray for Mrs. Smith. I pray, but not for Mrs. Smith. I am praying for that man in the sixth pew, the man with the balding hair, tan hat and dark suit. I want the pastor to lead the congregation to pray for this man, my father.

My father was worried about the people's reaction to his appearance. He needn't have worried. Only one or two people even said as much as hello to my dad. Why does the church seem so quiet? The hymns seem hollow. I don't know the tune and I'm not bothering to hide the fact."

After Dad died, my family fell apart. This book isn't a place for me to air family grievances. I won't comment further, only to say that my childhood was painful. There are plenty of other hardships to share that don't involve opening old wounds, so I'll move on to those.

I've been through a tornado, a blizzard, and a deep freeze of twenty-five degrees below freezing, actual temperature! I've survived nearly drowning in an ocean undertow when I was thirteen. I've beaten the odds and I've been granted a miracle over and over again.

I could have died when I was born blue as an infant. I could have died when I cracked my skull when I was a toddler. I could have died when I was in a childhood bicycle accident that left me sprawled on a gravel road just below the line of sight over a steep incline—I almost got run over by a car, but I didn't. Instead the driver of the car helped me. I could have died during my white water rafting accident, during my car accident, or during childbirth. There are many times when I really shouldn't have made it through, but I did.

And yet, instead of rejoicing over all of the times I've been saved, I've often felt sorry for myself. I can't point to any one hardship that crushed me. It's the totality of all of the dozens and dozens of hardships big and small, piling up, one after another, year after year, that made me cry out in anger and despair. "God, why am I cursed?"

We live in a hateful world. This world is not our home. This world is a dangerous and hostile place. And yet, day after day, most of us survive.

The world won't change for me. It will not get better. I can thrive anyway. Why am I here while so many others are gone? What can I do to live a life that expresses how grateful I am to be alive? How can I be grateful to be alive? I'm still here.

A successful life is like a pizza. It is a perfectly delicious circle, ready to enjoy with

159

the people we love. Each slice is part of a whole, and no slice should be too big or too small. Call one of the slices money. We need it for ourselves, and we need it to give to others in need. Label the other slices.

Healthy relationships? An education? A fulfilling job? Living our dreams? A nice house? Traveling the world? Doing things that scare us? Challenging ourselves? Label the slices in your pizza with these things and anything else that pops into your head.

Now I want you to imagine yourself eating the Success Pizza. Mmm, it sure is amazing, isn't it? How many slices did you imagine yourself eating? Did you eat the whole thing? Probably not. Who needs an entire pizza to feel satisfied? Unless we are gluttons, we are content after two or three slices, on average.

Life and success—it's your pizza. You don't need to have the whole thing all at once! **Thriving is when you know what you want, you understand what you need, and you**

are enjoying a few good slices at a time.
You'll have an entire pizza, but not at all at
once. And your pizza will be so much more
pleasurable if you share it with others.

That's what thriving means. It doesn't
mean perfection. It doesn't mean getting
everything we want all at once. It means
enjoying a few delicious slices at a time.

**Thriving is about being happy right
now, today, even if I can't have it all, even
if I have ongoing hardships.**

I am happy. I am happy no matter what.
And that's what thriving means.

NATALIE BUSKE THOMAS

9

GET OUT

My parents' last words to me were "Get out!" This is one of the most painful memories I carry with me. My parents died almost exactly twenty-five years to the day apart from each other. Dad was thirty-seven when he died from cancer. How could their last words to me be the same two horrible words: Get out? How? Why? Why didn't they

163

tell me that they loved me? Why did they use their last words to me to reject me?

My dad said these words in anguish. He yelled them. His voice was hoarse and strained. I've played the memory of it like an audio track that I can't delete. I've heard it over and over. Sometimes years will pass before I hear it. But then those words come back when something reminds me of that night.

He was lying there in his own bed, at home. Grandpa was there with him. Hospice was there. He was hooked up to machines. It was close to the end. Hospice had prepared the family that Dad was probably not going to make it through the night. He didn't. Before his last breath, and before the morphine gave him another round of relief, he saw me standing there, in the doorway of his room. He tried to sit up. He yelled, "Get out!" A few hours later he died while I was sleeping in the room that shared a wall with his. I was literally just a few feet away from him when he left this world while I was sleeping.

Fast forward twenty-five years. I'm all grown up now with children of my own. I'm Mom's caregiver. She is difficult. It is complicated. But no one can tell us that the love between us was wrong or not good enough. It was what we had, and it was strong enough for me to see her through to the end. It was strong enough to love her, no matter how hard it got.

Mom was home every day of her illness until the final day. She said that she almost died that morning, when I was out of town. She allowed us to take her to the hospital. What happened there is not something that I'm willing to talk about today. I'll skip ahead to her last words. She wasn't actually talking to me, she was talking to my husband. She was being moved for weighing and vital signs in her open-back hospital gown. She saw Brent standing in the doorway of the hospital room and she said to him that he'd have to "get out." I never heard my mother speak again. So, while her words weren't technically addressed to me, those were nonetheless the last words I heard her say: "Get out."

The odds of this happening at random are astronomical. I know without a doubt that this is no coincidence. What does it mean though? Why did my parents say those two words to me when they were leaving me? What does it all mean? Is it meant to harm me or help me? And if it's meant to help me, why can't I be helped in a loving and gentle way instead of in a painful and harsh way? Is this God's doing? Why me? Am I cursed?

My sixteen year old self believed that Dad didn't want me to see him suffering, and that he was upset to see me standing there, watching. Maybe he didn't want me to remember him that way. But I think there's more to it than that. There was something I was missing, something that I went my entire life not knowing.

When Mom uttered those same words "Get out", it was because she was losing her dignity. She was a private person. In the end, she never gave up her control. She didn't want to be embarrassed. She didn't want my husband to see her that way. She cared about what my husband thought of her. She thought of him as a son, not a son-in-law. She thought the world of him.

Maybe I was missing something. What else did "get out" mean to me? I realized that I heard those two words often. Grandma said this to me, but not when she was dying. She said it when she was full of life. She'd tell my cousins and me to get out when she wanted us to go outside and play. She'd say that we needed fresh air.

Grandma loved being outside. The backs of her hands were always brown because she hung her laundry out to dry even though she had a machine to do it for her. Whenever she noticed us lazing around the table, doing nothing, she'd stare at us. Then she'd tell us to get out. We never needed to be told twice!

We'd go out back and play on the bank where we'd made a rutted groove to slide down. Our moms would have a fit when they saw the filthy seat of our pants, but it was worth it. Sometimes we'd slip out with a few kitchen spoons to dig with. If Grandma later found them missing she always knew where to look—the bank.

Sometimes we threw crab apples at the nasty kids next door. They started it, of course. Other times we chased fireflies. When we were feeling brave we went over to the "crick". Grandma fussed the whole time we were getting ready to leave. We had to watch out for broken bottles. I can't remember the other warnings. I don't think I was listening.

But we all understood that when Grandma said "Get out", not only did she want us out of her hair, but she also meant for us to LIVE. Have an adventure. Do something scary. Do something fun. Get out there. And that's what my parents have always told me, too. *You are a smart girl, Natalie. Stop being such a chicken. Get out.*

Let's LIVE! Let's have adventures! Let's do something scary! That's what it means to thrive. Get out, live! **Thriving is to love life.**

But to love life, we must first learn how to love. People tell us that love is the answer. What does this mean specifically? How does love help us get ahead in life? How does love make us happy?

Bad things still happen and they keep piling on. Warm fuzzies won't chase the bad away. It's a hateful world. How does love help? Fortunately we have a definition that spells things out for us. Let's go back to that definition of love that I quoted earlier.

Love is patient.

Patience is one of the most important aspects of being a good parent. Patience is also beneficial in a marriage, at work, and in everything else. The larger the goal, the more patience is required. If you are like me and nearly all of your aspirations are of the longshot variety, you need patience. Entrepreneurs, small business owners, artists, writers, singers, musicians—all of you know what I mean by this.

Nearly every job requires training and sacrifice. **If you are patient, you won't quit when the going gets tough. You'll get what you want.** You'll eventually have that child, biologically or through adoption. You'll eventually get that mortgage. Whatever it is that you set out to do, if you have enough patience you'll have what it takes to work toward your goal until you reach it.

And when you are patient, you'll be more loving to everyone around you. People will love you back. You'll be happier not only when you've reached your goals, but along the way as well.

Have you ever watched a young child playing with small toy cars or little plastic animals? Children often line up their toys in a row. They patiently and methodically place the toys in an orderly way, even if the toys fall down or slip away repeatedly. They pick the toys back up and start over again as many times as it takes to get the job done. Children sometimes throw their toys in frustration when their plans fail, but many times they finish their task quietly and calmly. At the end of this laborious structuring of their toys, they say, "Come see what I did! Will you play with me?"

A life of patience allows us to get all of our work done so that we can play. I appreciate a day when I've been quietly and efficiently productive, like a child who has lined all of her toys in a row. I'm settled and ready to enjoy the day with my family. When I work through my day in an impatient and manic flurry, I'm scattered and stressed. More patience = more peace, better health, and a happier life.

Love is kind.

Kindness pays. Networking is when you do someone a favor with the expectation that they will return the favor. I'm not talking about backscratching. I'm talking about what some people call karma. *When you are kind to others, the world is kind to you.*

Love doesn't tear people down. If you are tempted to envy others, keep score, or delight when something bad happens to someone else, if you seek to take credit, if you promote yourself above others, if you do anything that isn't loving, well, you're hurting yourself. Hateful attitudes are a distraction from your life's purpose. You'll be caught up in the drama of these things and you'll lack the energy you need to succeed in the things that matter to you. Love focuses on raising people up, and therefore you'll raise yourself up as well.

The first Christmas after my mother died, I knew we'd have a hard time. My friends and relatives would be sharing their happy pictures and stories. I didn't want to feel resentful or wallow in self-pity when it was time to bring our kids to Nana's house. What would we do instead?

Even though it was hard for us to make a commitment to leaving our warm home on a bitterly cold Christmas morning, my husband and three children agreed that the best way to help ourselves through a lonely Christmas was to be kind to others. We volunteered at a free community lunch by signing up to provide entertainment. We loaded up the mini-van just after breakfast on Christmas morning with our guitars, dulcimers, jingle bells, and gear. We donned Santa hats and headed out the door, feeling rehearsed and confident, but also nervous.

Upon our arrival we entered into an awkward situation. A man dressed as Santa had shown up to perform during our scheduled timeslot, without a formal invitation. He was a local musician who plays for tips. No one knew how to handle the situation so we simply waited until he finished, through song after song after song. Our children hadn't had their Christmas yet, and it was asking a lot of them to spend so much time waiting for our turn. One of the event organizers stepped in to ask him to wrap things up. When he finally left, he took the sound system with him, as it had belonged to him.

Without microphones it was hard for anyone to hear us over the joyful din. All of our hours of practice had been for nothing! But how could we complain? Friends and strangers, elderly and babies, singles and families—the hall was decked with the Christmas spirit. Food was plentiful and the place was packed. So what if the chatter and laughter drowned us out.

But when were through with our set, there was a smattering of applause—from about five people. The folks sitting nearest to us were aglow, "We got a private concert!" The looks on their faces! We may have performed for just that one family, but it had been worth it.

We left the community dinner for home, humbled by the poor and the meek that we saw gathered there together. Our own modest stash of presents under the tree suddenly seemed richly blessed. Perception is everything! What had been a financially strained year had still left us with plenty of shiny presents and filled stockings. We were quiet as we stared at the tree in all of its glory. We had so much. We had all of this, and each other too.

We appreciated that Christmas more than we thought possible, and the loss of my mother was not as painful as we had feared it would be.

Love rejoices with the truth.

Don't lie. It will always come back to bite you. If nothing else, it will prevent you from thriving. People who rejoice in the truth sleep well at night. They have no reason to hide. They have nothing to fear. Whether it's in your relationships or in your career, honesty pays. Oh, it might not pay at first, and you might seethe when you see liars get what you rightfully deserved, but eventually, one day, everyone will know who to trust, and that person will be you.

But do lie when your elderly relative gives you a freezer burnt popsicle even though you are over forty and haven't had an orange popsicle in years, and have never liked them much to begin with! Say thank you and choke down every drop of icy food coloring on a stick. Kindness is more important than being a stickler for the truth. White lies of the harmless variety are kind.

It's the self-serving lies that are the problem:

Lies that avoid accountability.

Lies that get us ahead.

Lies that give us what we want.

Lies that serve our agenda.

Even if everything seems to turn out fine; the ends don't justify the means. The means always matter. One day, the truth will prevail and you'll want to be on the right side of it.

Love always protects.
Love always trusts.
Love always hopes.
Love always perseveres.

When you believe that everything will turn out the way that it was meant to be, you'll accept whatever comes your way. When you hope for the best, even if you expect the worst, you'll eventually succeed. Maybe it will take a long time. Love always perseveres. You will succeed if you conduct your life according to the definition of love.

Check your plans against the definition of love. If it all checks out, and your plans are honest, go for it. Get out! Don't be chicken. Give it a whirl. Love always trusts. Love always hopes. Go for it!

Never Give Up!

It's difficult to keep going when a business isn't doing as well as we'd like. It's hard not to throw in the towel when relationships are strained. Love perseveres. Fight for what you want, but be honest when something is over. Love rejoices in the truth.

When life piles on the challenges and the hardships are coming in fast and furious, one after another, remember that you aren't cursed. It's a hateful world, but you can thrive anyway. When you are hated choose to love anyway. I'm hardly the first person to tell you this, but maybe you need encouragement to stay true to what you already know.

I seek inspirational resources when I'm burned out and cynical. I read a variety of fiction and non-fiction for inspiration to stay focused on living my best life. Sometimes I inspire myself through my own writing, as it tends to take on a life of its own. I wrote this in *Ruby Red*, for my fictional time-traveling detective Serena Wilcox:

"I'm sorry. I'm having a hard time getting past this. All I know is that I felt a darkness that is hard to define. I never felt so worthless. I was despised and deemed redundant. Worst of all I was disposable. I was insignificant. I had no value. I was not worthy of living. Well, my God doesn't say so! I was specially formed in the womb to be born at a specific time. I serve a purpose. I have value. And I'm bound and determined to honor the incredible power that He has entrusted me with. I'm going to change history."

Unlike Serena Wilcox, you and I can't go back in time, but we can live in the present and have hope for the future. The advice I've given you is from the heart, and much of it isn't all that original. What I can add is another voice that tells you that love works. I'm thriving in a hateful world, and you can too. Anybody can. When the world chooses hate, we will choose love.

Create a Beautiful Life

I hated crayons. I hated the smell of them and the dreadful coloring books that accompanied them. I became an artist when I was a little girl sitting at the kitchen table with markers and blank sheets of paper. I loved the boldness of markers and the freedom of making my own lines.

These days art is part of my career. I lose all track of time when I'm immersed in an oil painting. The vivid colors on the palette are irresistible. I listen to Enya while I paint. Her music is hauntingly beautiful and dynamic. I was a dance student and then a dance teacher for most of my life. One of my greatest joys in dancing was choreography. Telling the story of music through dance—how can we experience music without dancing? I was sad when I needed to close my dance and theater business before a move. I thought my dancing days were over. My new career as an artist and an author seemed at first to be confining and lonely. Where was the joy? Where was the movement? Where was the dance?

Ah, but I had never done an oil painting before. I didn't realize. When I'm painting, I'm telling a story. And when I paint to music, I dance in color.

I love painting. I love what I do. I'm thrilled to share my art with the world. Create a beautiful life. Whatever it is that you were born to do, do it!

Beauty in general is an inspiration. I feel better when I look at flowers. I especially love to grow roses, but I have many favorites. I love butterfly gardens. Butterflies are on my list of inspirational beauty.

And who isn't captivated by hummingbirds? I used a free-standing shepherd's hook planter to bring hummingbirds to me. I grew flowers in the planter and hung a hummingbird feeder from the hook. My plan worked!

I've never seen a dolphin in the wild. That's on my list. I've seen dolphins in aquatic tanks at zoos and that's not the same thing at all. I want to see them swimming free. When I was a child I pretended that I was a dolphin whenever I was in a body of water. Haven't we all done that? None of us are all that different from each other. Some kinds of beauty are universally loved. Create a beautiful life by seeking beauty in nature, animals, art, people, and so much more. Photograph it, perform it, and share it! Beauty expands as you share it, and thriving comes naturally, even in an ugly world.

Have an Adventure

My family and I took a road trip to a city we've never been to before for a scheduled booksigning event. We entered the bookstore with our books, displayers, and bags. The bookstore owner kept us waiting. When she finally acknowledged us she was frosty. I asked where we should set up and she said, "where they just came from" (meaning the previous author and her entourage). Later she ambled over to where we were to warn us that there was no bathroom in the store. She then said, "There's no coffee because there's no bathroom."

I don't know what that means exactly, but it struck our funny bone. The signing was overall miserable, in ways that I can't mention because it violates my rules I dished out earlier in this book about venting. However, we had an adventure! We saw bison on the way to the event, during the event we spoke at great length to a most interesting person, and we picked up a new catch phrase.

We were exhausted. As soon as we got home from the event, after racing to the bathroom because we were of course in dire need by then, my husband made coffee. "There's a bathroom, so there's coffee." This will be a running joke for years to come.

I brought that up as an example of doing something outside of our comfort zone. It's not easy to go to an unfamiliar place, meet new people, and depend upon total strangers for your social and physical comfort. Sometimes the adventure goes awry and is an utter failure. I sold not a single book, and upon leaving, the bookstore owner declined to shelve any of my books. She held my books in her hands, flipped through them, made a sour expression, and then told me that no, no, she wouldn't be taking these on. I don't know how much more of failure that booksigning could have been! And yet, I'm glad we went. The experience added color to our lives. And looking back, the farce was hilarious.

Adventure in the more traditional sense conjures up an image of sleeping in a tent in the great outdoors, does it not? Ah, we've had those misadventures as well. There was the time when we were camping when it was unseasonably cold. Oh my, we were freezing! We had the campsite to ourselves, as we were apparently the only ones who ignored the weather report. It took us ages to fall asleep, but when we finally drifted off we were rudely awakened by the unmistakable sound of something munching on our tent. Deer had eaten a hole right through our tent lining!

We were wide awake then. Brent shone the car's headlights on the tent. We rushed to dismantle everything. We threw all of our stuff in the trunk and off we went, back home.

Another failed camping adventure involved sleeping with ticks during a tornado watch and a partial government shutdown that left us at a national park without a park ranger.

We sure know how to have a fun-filled family vacation! Oh, and did I mention that I was heavily pregnant at the time?

But what stories do we love to repeat until they become family classics? We've had many pleasant experiences in which everything went perfectly as planned. Those events were marvelous. It's a shame that I barely remember most of those occasions. No, it's the adventures that we remember the most. The hilarity, the mishaps, the excitement—these are the fabric of life. Have an adventure!

10

HELP

Are you inspired to thrive? Inspiration alone might not be enough. Sometimes I'm motivated to make big changes, but despite my best intentions I'm easily overwhelmed. Where do I begin? How long will this change take? I feel exhausted before I even get started. I quit before I do anything at all. Maybe tomorrow I'll dig in, maybe then.

I want to help you dig in *today*. I've been on my own for many years now. When my husband was in the Army I was alone for weeks at a time in a foreign country. I sometimes went several days without seeing a single person. This was before cell phones and the Internet. It was too expensive to call home more than once a week or so. I didn't even have TV. What did I do? How did I cope?

I learned how to get along with myself— but this lesson didn't come easily. At first I was proud of how independent I was. The fun of that wore off quickly. I was too young and undisciplined to handle solitude and I'm ashamed to say that I fell into lazy and slovenly habits. I stayed up late, I slept in late. I stayed in bed reading one book after another. I let the dishes pile up. I didn't have a dishwasher and I was weary of washing dishes by hand. Why work when no one would see the results anyway?

One dark day my German landlords came upstairs and knocked on my door. What did they want? They never came up. I opened the door and they marched on through, down the tiny hall and into the tiny kitchen. They bent their heads as they were both quite tall and the attic ceiling was slanted. I was embarrassed to be caught with such a sty. I liked and respected these kind people. What did they think of this mess?

They let me know, loudly. I wished I couldn't understand them, but I got the gist of it. I heard "schmutzig" (dirty) and a lot of "nein, nein" and "nicht gut". As if the message wasn't already clear enough, they hammered the point home with gestures. I assured them that I'd clean the apartment. And I did. Not only did I pull myself together that day, but I kept myself together for the rest of my life (most of the time).

I realized that day that I never want to be in that sorry state of affairs ever again. Shouldn't my life be in order even if no one is watching me? A schmutzig house is a dirty house even if I'm the only one in it. When I need motivation to get my act together, I imagine an angry German lady standing over me, "Nicht gut! Nein, nein, nein!"

Sometimes I'm broken and I need a gentler approach. When I was a child I stayed the night at my cousin's home. In the morning, my aunt brushed Jennifer's hair and then mine. Jennifer had naturally curly hair and a tender scalp. My aunt had the patience of a saint as she brushed my cousin's curls amid whining and fussing and much drama. Next, it was my turn.

I expected a rough hand. My own mom was as different from her sister as she could have possibly been. She was impatient and easily frustrated. Brushing my hair sometimes caused my scalp to bleed. My head jerked backward with her harsh strokes. I knew better than to complain. I always gritted my teeth until the ordeal was over.

I expected the same treatment from my aunt. After all, Jennifer had carried on so much. It was going to be terrible, I just knew it! I steeled myself up for the experience.

Why hadn't she started already? I wanted to get this over with. I felt only a whisper on the back of my head. I turned around to see what was going on. My aunt said, "Am I hurting you?"

I think of that whenever I need to go easier on myself. Jennifer's hair was gorgeous, all the time. That morning my hair was also neat and pretty. A soft touch can be just as effective and much more loving. The job may have taken longer, but I was so grateful for the tenderness and mercy.

When I'm wallowing in self-pity I need the angry German landlord approach. And when I'm broken I need a whisper in my hair. But for my everyday self, here are some habits that help me thrive. I can't keep up with all ten of these things every day. I do what I can. When life derails me I get back on track as soon as can. My dear friend Kelly told me yesterday that I "bloom where I am planted". That's all we can do.

Try just one or two new ideas at a time. Substitute your own ideas, like spending time with animals (riding horses, walking a dog, etc.) or spending time outdoors. Stick with the ideas that work until they become habits. Too much at once is overwhelming.

Thriving doesn't mean perfection. I'm not always a perky overachiever, and I can't always follow my own best advice, but I can put one foot in front of the other, one day at a time. Some days are more joyful than others. Deep down, happiness rests inside me even when my days are dark. I thrive when I'm at peace, and so can you.

10 Habits for Thriving

1

Wear your shoes.

This is an easy thing that you can do right away. When I'm in bare feet, slippers or socks, I move slowly. If I wear athletic shoes I move faster. I have a lift to my steps and I get more work done. This works especially well if I need to sweep the floors and finish other active chores. Try it! Keep a clean pair of shoes to wear inside your home.

2

Keep a dry-erase calendar.

I have a magnetic one month calendar on my fridge. I write appointments on the dates. Each morning I put an X on yesterday's box. At the end of the month I erase the whole thing. There's something freeing about wiping the slate clean.

3

Listen more, talk less.

Most of my stress is due to people. When I need a break, I stop talking. I listen. I sit back. I let others talk. If there is nothing else you take away from these tips, I hope you try this one. Talking invites a response. If you need a break, don't talk. Also, when you listen, you'll learn more about the people around you. Certain things will become clear to you when you do this. It'll be easier to know what to do to improve or let go of your relationships. I surprise myself when I'm content to be still and let others speak. This helps me feel kinder and therefore become kinder. Kindness is love, and love always perseveres. Listening is a simple choice that leads to powerful change.

4

Don't answer the phone.

Whether it's a telemarketer or a friend, the person on the other end of the line has the upper hand while I'm caught unaware. I used to jump whenever the phone rang. I'd say "yes" when people asked me to volunteer for something. I'd let others derail my day. They'd call to vent about their problems and the next thing I knew, the afternoon was shot. I'd listen, believing that I was meant to drop whatever it was that I was doing to help them. I now feel that this type of behavior was enabling the other person while harming myself. I realized that it was never me in particular they wanted, just anyone who picked up the phone! Goodness, I fell for that trap far too many times.

They've stopped calling me altogether now. I'm always willing to make time for people who really do need me— that hasn't changed. My friends send me e-mail or an instant message when they want to talk. I should have set boundaries a long time ago. For the past few years I've let my calls go to voice mail and it's made all the difference. What peace I have, knowing that my day won't go off course every time the phone rings!

5

Be willing to do the work.

It's going to take effort to thrive. The good life doesn't come easily. Take painting, for example. I have to shop for supplies. I have to set up an easel and canvas. I have to decide what to paint. When I'm done with my painting session I have to clean up. What a lot of work that is! Why do it at all? Because I want to live! I want to work hard and play hard. I only get one go at this life, only one round. The work is worth doing. I break the work up into smaller chunks. Sometimes it's helpful if I set up for painting one day and paint the next. I also found a paintbrush cleaner that makes cleanup much easier, without any toxic fumes. A little research about how to make work lighter can be a big help. Whatever it is that you want to do, be willing to do the work. You won't regret it!

6

Slow down.

I'm much more productive and in control when I slow down. When I make a special meal for my family I break out the good stuff, even if it's just an ordinary day. I take my time when I'm cooking. I add a dash here, a splash there, a sizzle here. The day settles over me while I prepare the food. I digest the day's events. When the meal is ready, I eat slowly. I chew each bite to savor the flavors. Eating is a delightful experience! I so love food! I enjoy each bite completely, which is why I'm usually content without overindulging. When my stomach keeps up with what I'm putting in it I feel full. It's easier to stop eating when I'm satisfied. A healthy me is a high energy me. I apply this slowness to many other aspects of my day. Doing things in a deliberate and conscious way brings awareness and peace to what I'm doing. Whenever I find myself zipping mindlessly through the day I make an effort to slow down. Racing around might seem faster but how can I thrive if I'm detached from my life?

7

Structure your days.

Do your best to go to sleep at the same time every night, and rise at the same time every morning. You'll know that you've made a natural habit of this when you struggle to stay awake when your bedtime arrives, and when you fall asleep fairly easily. You'll wake without an alarm clock and you'll feel ready for the day much sooner than when you are forced awake before your body is refreshed. Sleep is a precious commodity. Discipline yourself to go to bed on time and wake on time, even on the weekends. I'm a reformed night owl. Mornings are my favorite time of day, but then again I have many favorite times of the day. That's the point: get more sleep and you'll enjoy your life more!

8

Dance!

I need to move. I need to be fit. I need to feel music. I need to dance! Sometimes I fall into a season of sloth in which I hardly move from the computer chair to the bed and back again. I miss being physical and full of energy when I'm sedentary too long. Dancing is joyful. It is praise. The mind and spirit benefit from a healthy body. Even if struggling with disability, we can dance by merely clapping our hands. Babies dance. We were born that way! Somewhere along the way, we felt that we needed permission to dance. We dance if we are at a wedding reception. We *might* dance if no one is watching. I challenge you to dance more. You might even want to take a dance class. If you haven't danced in a while, you may surprise yourself by how much you enjoy it.

9

Sing!

Sing or play an instrument—become an active participant in music. Music is everything! There's not an emotion we can have that hasn't already been expressed in music. Listening to music is not enough. I challenge you to become a part of it. If you've always wanted to learn how to play an instrument and haven't, do it now. Beginner instruments are inexpensive. There's a plethora of free tutorials online. Do you already play but you haven't done anything with it in a while? Make the time.

10

Pray.

When I don't know what to do, I pray. When I need inspiration for a painting I pray. When I am afraid, I pray. I pray when I know someone is hurting. I pray when I'm hurting. I pray every day, throughout the day. A praying person is a hopeful person. A praying person believes that a Higher Power sees and cares. A praying person has faith.

I prayed before my parents died. I prayed while they were dying. I prayed after they died. I prayed during my white water rafting accident and afterward. I prayed when I couldn't conceive. I prayed when I was in labor. I prayed after the baby was born. I kept on praying as each of my three babies grew. I'll never stop praying.

If you aren't a praying person, you might say, "What good did your praying do? Your parents died anyway." I know that prayer isn't going to save me from hardship, not usually anyway. Miracles do happen, I'm not discounting it. I'm only trying to explain that when I pray, I don't expect a physical result as much as a spiritual one.

Largely, the world itself moves along on its course, with or without my prayers. But when I pray, I invite peace into my life. I gain wisdom. I think my earlier analogy about faith being like falling in love is a good one to reference. How do we know that we want to spend the rest of our life with someone? The whole idea sounds ludicrous! Why should *anyone* marry? Yet people do. And many of us stay married to the same person until the end.

Prayer connects me with God. It gives me peace, hope, wisdom, strength, and the ability to act in love when I don't want to. I hope that you've experienced the beauty of prayer for yourself. If you haven't, I challenge you to be open to the possibility.

It hurts when this world is hateful. When people place ideology ahead of caring about the needs of the individual, it hurts. When people oppress us, it hurts. We can use all the help we can get!

I long to be free, to make my own choices, follow my dreams and believe as I wish. People may try to keep me down but I won't let them. They may choose hate, but I will choose love. The world is hateful but I thrive anyway. And so can you.

ABOUT THE AUTHOR

Natalie loves all things Irish, oil painting, sugar cookies, the color red, pizza, live music, and singing. She is an author of books for all ages and enjoys people who are still capable of having an imagination, of having a sense of wonder, of feeling hopeful and full of energy, of feeling as if anything is possible, of feeling afraid of scary things and unafraid of the rest... of having courage, of being selfless, of being spontaneous, of recognizing humor, and of living life to the absolute fullest.

Natalie was born in upstate New York, raised in Indiana, and then lived in Germany for three years. She currently resides near the Twin Cities (Minneapolis, Saint Paul, Minnesota). Natalie would one day like to time travel, but for now she writes about it.

Visit Natalie's website to view her oil
paintings and to enjoy free bonus material.
www.NatalieBuskeThomas.com

If you enjoyed this book, please tell
your friends and family about it.
Thank you.

www.ingramcontent.com/pod-product-compliance
Lightning Source LLC
Chambersburg PA
CBHW032002060426
42446CB00041B/1035